Let us bless the Lord

Let us bless the Lord

Rediscovering the Old Testament
through Psalm 103

Stephen B. Dawes

British Library Cataloguing in Publication data

A catalogue record for this book is available from the British Library

ISBN 1 85852 287 0

First published by Inspire
4 John Wesley Road
Werrington
Peterborough PE4 6ZP

Printed and bound in Great Britain by
William Clowes Ltd, Beccles, Suffolk

Contents

Introduction

The Old Testament, God and Psalm 103

Marcion was a very active Christian missionary and church leader in Rome in the second century, and he had strong views about the Old Testament and its god. He didn't think that the Old Testament should be Christian Scripture at all; and he didn't think that the god of the Old Testament was the God and Father of our Lord Jesus Christ. He saw the Old Testament as an outdated and barbaric book; and he believed that the god of the Old Testament was a cruel and thoroughly unpleasant god, greatly inferior to the God of Love made known to the world by Jesus. Although Marcion and his followers were excommunicated as heretics in 144, his views were very popular in the churches of his day and his legacy remains with us. He lives on as a shadowy presence in the Church, whispering insidiously about the Nasty God of the Old Testament and the Nice One of the New, with the result that that way of thinking about the Old Testament and its god is widely, even if unofficially, held today.

I must admit that Marcion had a point. The Old Testament is a very large anthology of ancient religious literature, some of which is pretty unreadable and some of which is unquestionably offensive, although both of these things can be said of parts of the New Testament too. Although I can certainly understand why the Old Testament is a largely unopened book as far as the Church today is concerned, I cannot leave it there. So be warned. This book is written in the conviction that although the Old Testament is an ancient library from a strange culture, and despite the fact that it is long, complicated and at times both utterly tedious and

1

downright repugnant, it is nevertheless worth staying with if we want to think about 'God' and 'the meaning of life, the universe and everything'. Marcion had a point, but so did the mainstream Church leaders who decided that he was wrong.

A very good place to see just how wrong Marcion is about the God of the Old Testament, and why the Old Testament as a whole really is worth staying with, is Psalm 103, and the teaching of that psalm forms the core of this book. It is my 'desert-island psalm'. If I was allowed only one chapter from the Old Testament on my desert island, then this would be it. If I was allowed only two chapters from the whole Bible, then Psalm 103 would be one of them (the other would be the last part of Romans 8). This ancient hymn from the Temple in Jerusalem is an excellent summary of everything that is best in the whole Bible, not just the Old Testament. Almost everything that needs to be said about God is there, and the only bit that needs to be added is to say that everything said in that psalm about God is subsequently repeated, re-emphasized and lived out in the life and teaching of Jesus of Nazareth.

Psalm 103 Of David

1. Bless the LORD, O my soul,
       and all that is within me,
       bless his holy name.
2. Bless the LORD, O my soul,
       and do not forget all his benefits –
3. who forgives all your iniquity,
       who heals all your diseases,
4. who redeems your life from the Pit,
       who crowns you with steadfast love and
       mercy,
5. who satisfies you with good as long as you live
       so that your youth is renewed like the
       eagle's.

6. The LORD works vindication
      and justice for all who are oppressed.
7. He made known his ways to Moses,
      his acts to the people of Israel.
8. The LORD is merciful and gracious,
      slow to anger and abounding in steadfast
         love.
9. He will not always accuse,
      nor will he keep his anger for ever.
10. He does not deal with us according to our
         sins,
      nor repay us according to our iniquities.
11. For as the heavens are high above the earth,
      so great is his steadfast love towards those
         who fear him;
12. as far as the east is from the west,
      so far he removes our transgressions from
         us.
13. As a father has compassion for his children,
      so the LORD has compassion for those who
         fear him.
14. For he knows how we were made;
      he remembers that we are dust.

15. As for mortals, their days are like grass;
      they flourish like a flower of the field;
16. for the wind passes over it, and it is gone,
      and its place knows it no more.
17. But the steadfast love of the LORD   4 x
      is from everlasting to everlasting
      on those who fear him,
      and his righteousness to children's children,
18. to those who keep his covenant
      and remember to do his commandments.

19. The LORD has established his throne in the
         heavens,
      and his kingdom rules over all.

20. Bless the LORD, O you his angels,
      you mighty ones who do his bidding,
      obedient to his spoken word.
21. Bless the LORD, all his hosts,
      his ministers that do his will.
22. Bless the LORD, all his works,
      in all places of his dominion.
      Bless the LORD, O my soul.

Psalm 103 begins and ends with the call to 'bless the LORD', which is to acknowledge that of all the gods on offer it is the LORD alone who is God and who is the source of life and blessing. It ends with a call to the whole universe to give the LORD the recognition which is his due. In fact, the psalm begins and ends in much the same way as the Lord's Prayer begins and ends, and in its first and last words – 'Bless the LORD, my soul' – those who sing or pray the psalm are invited to make that acknowledgement their own as the basis of their living, thinking and acting.

The kernel of the psalm repeats a mini-creed running right through the Old Testament which celebrates God's *steadfast love* and *mercy*, his *righteousness* and *justice*. These are very important words in the Old Testament, and they are lovely, warm words there. They speak of a love which will not let us go, but which seeks us out with kindness and embraces us with generosity. They speak of a new-every-morning sort of love, which takes our sins, our mistakes and all the sad and sorry failures of our lives and puts them behind us. God's *righteousness* is his love yearning and working to put things right; and his *justice* is his love in action to restore things to how they ought to be. So, when the Old Testament speaks about God as our *judge* it doesn't picture him as the impartial and unbending judges of our courts, but as the one who springs to our aid to sort everything out and make it right again. If we confuse that Old

Testament meaning with the modern one, as so much Christian thinking does, then we get things seriously wrong: but if we stay with this psalm, we avoid that pitfall. Here is a God who is generously kind and utterly reliable, our 'Covenant God' who wants to be involved with us and who stays by us despite our failings. Yes, this God gets *angry* too, but it's the anger of a loving and committed parent, whose anger, frustration and the tears in which they show themselves are a mark of love. There is nothing here which says that God's anger is his normal emotion towards us, that we are sinners and deserve it, that we have offended against God's justice and so he has no alternative but to punish us. Instead, the psalm says that God deals with our sin by forgiving it. And why? Because he's like that! Psalm 103 is my Old Testament-in-a-nutshell psalm. It is simple, sane and humane; but profound in what it says about God, faith and life.

In this book, and starting from Psalm 103, I shall be asking only one kind of question about the Old Testament – what has it to say to us about God, life and ourselves? This is a theological question, for whatever else it is or whatever its different books look like, the Old Testament is a Library of Theology. It is, admittedly, not an easy read, nor does it speak with one voice; but what holds it together and makes it worth taking the trouble to read is its subject matter. It is about God and it is about the meaning of life. It was written out of the struggles of real people to discover God and to believe in him; although we should probably also say that it was written out of God's struggle to make himself known, to let himself be found, and to save his world. Either way, it was written that others might come to share a vision of God, his will and his ways and so it comes to us 'from faith and for faith', to use a phrase from St Paul. It is a book of testimonies of individuals and groups to what they believed God had done for them, to what they thought he was like, and to how they felt they ought therefore to live as his people; and in it an invitation also comes to us to believe and to live.

Psalm 103, with its clear message about God and faith and life, is not only a good place to see how wrong many prejudices against the Old Testament and its God really are; it is a good way into the Old Testament as a whole. It is, after all, a psalm; and even if much of the Old Testament is a closed book in churches today, we still use psalms in worship. They might not be sung in their traditional form as much as they once were, but they are still being printed in hymn books so that they can be read responsively. And old favourite hymns like 'The Lord's my shepherd' (Psalm 23), 'All people that on earth do dwell' (Psalm 100) and 'Let us with a gladsome mind' (Psalm 136) are being joined by new songs like 'Jubilate' (also Psalm 100), 'From the rising of the sun' (Psalm 113) and 'Hear my cry, O God' (Psalm 61), as well as by numerous choruses which are simple repetitions of verses from the psalms, to keep the book of Psalms alive in our worship. Psalm 103 itself is represented in most hymn books by Henry Francis Lyte's hymn of 1834, 'Praise my soul, the King of heaven'.

But there is more to it than that. While we are still vaguely familiar with the words, ideas and images of some of the psalms, we also know how to use them, for we know what to do with hymns or worship songs. They might be more important in some churches than others, but most churches have recognized that music and song are powerful media for worship and spirituality. To sing one's faith is to impress it in the memory and send it deep into the unconscious. And so, given that hymns are poetry, filled with images and allusions, symbols and pictures, when this poetry is sung it feeds the soul and the imagination, engages the emotions and stirs the will. And when we sing we are also joined to other singers past and present. Hymns and worship songs give a worshipping community the chance to express its faith, to be reminded of important parts of it and to be strengthened in it. They bind people together with generations which have gone before, as they retell the 'old, old story' of faith which gives meaning to lives. They focus theology for devotional use and give congregations words of faith for worship. The Book of Psalms does exactly that for the theology of the Old Testament and for the faith of Israel, and Psalm 103 does it for the Book of Psalms as a whole. Here are words of worship and of faith, theology in poetry, inviting us to sing and respond.

Questions for reflection

1. What do you think about Marcion's views? Are they still to be found today?

2. Are there any passages from the Old Testament in your 'desert island Bible'? If there are – what is it about them which you value? If there aren't – why do you think this is?

3. What are your reactions to reading Psalm 103 in this chapter?

4. What words would you choose to describe the 'God of the Old Testament'?

1

A God of blessing

'Generous' is not an adjective that most people would choose if they were asked for words to describe the God of the Old Testament. 'Harsh' and 'vengeful' and other negative terms are much more likely to be suggested, given the severe image-problem that the Old Testament has both inside and outside the churches. 'Generous' is, however, a very good adjective to describe God as he is pictured in Psalm 103 and, though we don't usually think so, in much of the rest of the Old Testament too.

Psalm 103 begins with a call to worship God, but we'll leave what it means to worship God and to 'bless the LORD' until chapter 6, and go straight into the list of generous gifts for which the psalm calls us to praise, thank or 'bless' the LORD, their giver. According to the psalmist we are to give honour and worship to God because we live by his amazing generosity. God is 'the Lord and Giver of Life'. He is the one 'from whom all blessings flow'. He is 'the giver of every good and perfect gift'. The psalm insists that human beings are richly blessed by a generous God from whom life comes as a gift.

At the same time, we can also see from the way he puts it that the psalmist knows what human beings are like. 'Do not forget all his benefits,' he says, knowing that taking things for granted is a common human weakness, and that we are all prone to take great benefits with little thanks. 'Take care that you do not forget what God has done for you' is one of the constant themes of Deuteronomy (e.g. 4.9, 6.12, 8.11-19), and these verses, and indeed this psalm, warn us against not just those things that slip our minds, but about the way we ignore God and fail to thank him for the good things of life.

Verses 2-5 spell out the reason for voicing our gratitude for God's generous goodness and give examples of it. The LORD is the one

−ve
  who forgives all your iniquity,
  who heals all your diseases,
  who redeems your life from the Pit,

+ve
  who crowns you with steadfast love and mercy,
  who satisfies you with good as long as you live
  so that your youth is renewed like the eagle's.

The first three examples are taken from the negative side of human experience, and God's generosity is seen in the way he rescues us from the shadow side of life, from 'iniquity', disease and death. The others are from positive aspects of life in which God's goodness is seen in the joys and strengths of life itself. Together they reinforce our sense of God's generous goodness, point out our dependence on it and evoke our gratitude for it. God's love has entered into every part of the psalmist's life: he has been forgiven, healed, redeemed, crowned, satisfied and renewed. 'All' of these benefits from God are to be remembered, for 'all' of his sins have been forgiven and 'all' of his illnesses healed. So he acknowledges that he should praise God with 'all' that is in him. It is not enough to praise God only with our lips, or with only an outward gesture, it has to come from within, from the depths of our being. The psalm states boldly at the beginning that because God's goodness and generosity is total, our gratitude and commitment should be too.

In a way, each of these reasons for blessing the LORD is to do with health and healing. They point to God as the Lord and Giver of Life who gives wholeness of life to the psalmist, an idea that was as important in the faith of ancient Israel as it has been to all people everywhere, and as it is to us. In the book of Psalms we find two main types of psalms, Laments, which are prayers to God for help and Praises, which are thanksgivings for help received, and the subject of both types is very often that of health, either personal health in one way or another, or the health and well-being of the nation. These ancient hymns see God as the 'Lord of Life and Conqueror of Death', whose help is to be sought in maintaining wholeness and in combating disease.

Health is obviously important. As long as we've got our health, we say; that's the most important thing in life. We know when we think about it a bit further that that is not quite true, for when we lose a loved one we know what really matters most to us. Also we all know people who actually don't enjoy good health for one reason or another yet whose lives are rich, complete and happy. Nevertheless the importance of our health is undeniable, exactly as it was to the people of Israel and their psalmists, and it is therefore natural that health is seen as one of God's gifts. God is the God of Life, and recovery from sickness is part of God's generous and life-giving work in our lives, to be prayed for or given thanks for in worship.

We have very little idea about health in ancient Israel or about its health care services. A list of illnesses mentioned in the Old Testament would do little more than state the obvious fact that illness and sickness of one sort or another existed then as now. Most healing then seems to have depended on what we would call 'folk-medicine', where cures and remedies were based on long and careful observation. There was also a very close link between religion and medicine, and the role of the local sanctuary and its priest or holy man or woman was important. We do know that many in Israel believed that suffering was the result of sin, and that sickness was a punishment from God. We can see that in Psalm 103.3 where 'forgives all your iniquity' is paired with 'heals all your diseases', and that way of understanding suffering is clearly expressed in the teaching of Deuteronomy, where God offers his chosen people a choice: they may choose to honour him and walk in his ways, or they may choose to please themselves. If they choose to follow him they will be blessed, but if they choose to go their own way they will suffer. Nowhere is this more starkly put than in Deuteronomy 30.15-20, especially in verse 19:

> 'I call heaven and earth to witness against you today that I have set before you life and death, blessings and curses. Choose life so that you and your descendants may live ...'.

So when Job in the fable loses his prosperity, his children die, and he is in agony from disease, it is natural that his friends tell him that it is because he has sinned. What he must do is admit this, they say, and ask for God's forgiveness; then he will be restored to full health and prosperity. The book of Job goes on to object most strongly that it is not as simple as this, that at times the innocent suffer, and that illness is not necessarily the consequence of sin, a point made also in Habakkuk.

Although there was an alternative view that suffering was not the will of God, but was caused by evil spirits, or by the power of evil, and so it was possible for innocent and good people to suffer, nevertheless most of the Old Testament sees a clear link between sin and suffering and this idea is still found today. The angry or painful question that we have all heard, 'What have I done to deserve this?'

when illness, tragedy or suffering strikes, goes back in a straight line to these old beliefs that suffering is the result of sin. Those who say it usually share Job's defiance that in fact they have not done anything to deserve it at all, but the idea is still there that illness and sin are somehow related. There is, of course, sufficient truth in the idea for it to be credible, and in the right place it conveys a warning that needs to be heard. But in the wrong place, which is the vast majority of cases of personal illness and suffering, it is a very dangerous idea that has caused and still can cause considerable unnecessary anguish.

In Psalm 103.3 the psalmist praises God for forgiveness and for healing, and we'll look specifically at the big questions of sin and forgiveness in chapter 4. Whatever the cause of his suffering may have been he recognizes that every healing, every recovery, every victory over suffering comes from God and is part of his work. And in the next verse, the psalmist praises God for saving him from death, for 'the Pit' is the Pit of Death, or *Sheol* as it is sometimes called in other psalms. The psalmist doesn't live in a fool's paradise, where everything in the garden is lovely. He knows that there is a shadow side to life, and that death belongs to it, even epitomizes it.

There are two different ways of looking at death in the Old Testament. One is where death comes at its proper time, when someone dies peacefully in old age having lived out their 70 or 80 years. Here those who die are 'gathered to their people', and their relatives, though grieving, can rejoice over a life 'faithfully lived and peacefully died'. So 'Abraham breathed his last and died in a good old age, an old man and full of years, and was gathered to his people' (Genesis 25.8). His sons bury him and life goes on. St Francis of Assisi can sing of death in a similar way:

And thou, most kind and gentle death,
Waiting to hush our latest breath,
O praise him, alleluia!
Thou leadest home the child of God,
And Christ our Lord the way has trod:
O praise him, Alleluia!

But there is another side to death which is vicious, terrifying and completely negative. Death is the great enemy. It leads those forces of evil which are always trying to destroy, hurt and deface what is beautiful, good and healthy. Death is a dangerous monster living in a pit, who is always trying to reach out and catch passers-by with its tentacles and drag them down into darkness and destruction, drowning them in its watery cavern. So illness, disaster and suffering of any kind are symptoms of death trying to get its grip on the living, as can be seen in Psalm 18.4-5:

The cords of death encompassed me;
the torrents of perdition assailed me;
the cords of Sheol entangled me;
the snares of death confronted me.

But the psalmist goes on to testify:

In my distress I called upon the LORD;
to my God I cried for help.
From his temple he heard my voice,
and my cry to him reached his ears. (v. 6)

He reached down from on high, he took me;
he drew me out of mighty waters. (v. 16)

Death is a terrible pit, with miry clay and deep water to drown the one who falls or is dragged into it. But God can save us from it, because he is powerful love, goodness and life in permanent opposition to this malice, evil and death. He is the one who 'redeems' people from these things. 'Redeems' is an old-fashioned sort of word, and people might dismiss it on that score, but it is an important idea in the Old Testament. If hard times fell on a family, and they faced eviction from their land, or were forced to sell themselves into slavery in order to survive, then the next of kin had the responsibility of coming to their aid. He was their 'redeemer', their 'protector' and it was his responsibility to help them, if necessary by taking over their debts, buying back their land, or, if the worse had come to the worst, buying them out of slavery. There is a good example of this in the short novel about Naomi and Ruth. Naomi and her husband had gone as economic migrants to Moab because of famine in Judah, then Naomi is widowed and decides to return home. Back at Bethlehem she encourages her daughter-in-law, Ruth, a Moabite who is now also a widow, to make herself known to their wealthy kinsman, Boaz. There is a nearer relative but he is not prepared to take on his proper responsibility as 'redeemer', so Boaz 'redeems' Naomi and also marries Ruth (Ruth 4).

So the meaning of Psalm 103.4 is plain: God saves, rescues, delivers us from this shadow side of life. He is our 'redeemer', protector, saviour, deliverer and liberator. God is on the side of life, he is supremely the 'Lord of Life and Conqueror of Death', or 'our help in every time of trouble' as we say in funeral services. This positive and confident attitude is seen in the popular Jewish toast and greeting, *'leChayim'*, 'To Life'. In that word with its hope and defiance of death, there is a whole creed and celebration of the victory of God over death, no matter how strong, terrifying and real the forces of death seem to be.

The psalm then goes on to celebrate the fact that 'The LORD is the one who satisfies you with good as long as you live'. What is this 'good' with which God has filled the psalmist's life? We might think that the psalmist is praising God here for forgiveness and new life, with all the spiritual blessings of knowing the love of God, and no doubt that is part of what the psalmist means. But we must not overlook the way the psalmist appreciates the gifts of good *things* as well, for the Old Testament has a very positive approach to life and it is not ashamed of 'things'. It celebrates the goodness of life and of the material world. It is a great thing to be alive and to be human. The world is good, and its blessings are to be enjoyed, as in that toast.

We see this clearly in the first of the Old Testament's four creation pictures, the one in Genesis 1.1–2.4. God creates the world in seven days, and at some point in the account of every day's work, except for Day Two, the story says that God 'saw that it was good', and when he looks back at the end of all his work he sees that it was 'very good' (Genesis 1.31). We see the same in Psalm 8 which praises God as the King of Creation, and in the Harvest Psalm, Psalm 104, which fills out the picture. Human life is good, and God is to be thanked because he causes the grass to grow for the cattle and plants for us:

> to bring forth food from the earth,
> and wine to gladden the human heart,
> oil to make the face shine,
> and bread to strengthen the human heart. (Psalm 104.14-15)

The Old Testament celebrates life and the world. Even Ecclesiastes, with its dreary beginning 'Vanity of vanities, all is vanity' and the pessimism that runs through many of its pages, can still say that the meaning of life is to be found in taking life's pleasures when they come, 'Eat, drink and be merry' (8.15 in the Authorized Version, and also 2.24, 3.13, 5.18 and

9.7). Then there is the Song of Songs which is a vibrant and explicit celebration of human sexuality, sensual and unashamed. This is all part of the Old Testament's positive attitude to life and to the world in general, including material things. Life is the gift of God, and he is a bounteous giver. Life is good, sex is good, food and drink are good: they are given to be enjoyed. Of course, the Old Testament is also aware of the dangers in this. Feasting can become gluttony. My feasting can mean that others starve. Enjoyment of the good things of life can encourage greed and covetousness, theft and murder. Irresponsible sex can lead to misery, natural drives unchecked to rape. Life is good, but the world needs to be safeguarded from extremes and dangers, and its most dangerous creature is the human one. Hence the rules and guidelines that the Old Testament contains, for the benefit of all and the protection of the vulnerable.

The second creation picture in Genesis 2–3 highlights these dangers, and ends with the scene of God's good creation spoiled by the tensions between humans and animals, men and women, humans and the earth itself, and between humanity and their God. All is not right in the good world that God has made, and the Old Testament knows the reality of sin and evil and its power and of a world marred by conflict, terror and pain. At the same time it does not believe that these dreadful realities will have the last word. That, it teaches, lies with God who will eventually put all things right. And one of the pictures it uses for this good time to come illustrates just how positive the Old Testament is about 'things':

> On this mountain the LORD of hosts will make for all peoples a feast of rich food, a feast of well-matured wines, of rich food filled with marrow, of well-matured wines strained clear. (Isaiah 25.6)

Here is recognition of the good things of life, of feasting and laughter, joy and delight, to be celebrated and enjoyed. This is where the picture of 'the heavenly banquet prepared for all people' comes from which is used at the end of some Communion services.

There is nothing here at all, however, about any life after death. The psalmist is content with his life on earth, and if it is long and happy that is everything he can wish for. At the end of such a life he can die content and happy. There is in fact no clear idea of any real life after death in the Old Testament, other than a gradual fading into oblivion in *Sheol*, until we read in its last book to be written:

> Many of those who sleep in the dust of
> the earth shall awake, some to everlasting
> life, and some to shame and everlasting
> contempt. (Daniel 12.2)

This bold statement of a belief in life after death can be dated to around 165 BC in the course of the Maccabean War. At the time of Jesus nearly 200 years later this doctrine of the resurrection of the dead was still contentious. The conservative Sadducees refused to believe in this piece of new-fangled theology, which the Pharisees, followed by the Christians, firmly believed (Mark 12.18-27, Acts 23.6-10).

So our psalmist's horizon is death. For him this life is all. He knows that it will inevitably and all too quickly come to an end (vv. 14-16): but for the life that he has been given and all its good things he is grateful. God has filled his life with good things, and as a result his 'youth is renewed like the eagle's', a proverbial and vivid image of effortless stamina and soaring freedom. With this vivid picture the psalmist rounds off his list of the benefits for which a generous

God is to be blessed. The LORD of Life has given him health, strength and vitality, and for that he is to be acknowledged as God, praised and thanked. God has been amazingly generous, and our praise is our response to that generosity. The psalmist knows that life is not perfect, but insists that there is more than enough that is good to evoke our gratitude. He doesn't want to bribe us into praising God in order that God may bless us, instead he invites us to praise God as we look back on God's goodness towards us.

There is in this psalm, as there is in much of the Old Testament, a considerable element of 'good news', of 'gospel', about God's gracious love and care demonstrated in all kinds of ways. We do not need to wait until the first chapter of the New Testament to read about the acts of a caring God in helping his people, and 'saving' them from their sins and themselves. Psalm 103 demonstrates that the Old Testament is well aware of a God who takes initiatives of love, and that all religion, all worship, all good behaviour is a response to what God has already done. At the beginning of the Ten Commandments, the same point is made powerfully. The Israelites are addressed by the God who has already freed them from Egypt, who now gives them these commandments so that they can continue to enjoy the freedom and new life which he has given them (Exodus 20.2). We see this too in the way that the Old Testament begins with stories of creation, that 'In the beginning God created the heavens and the earth', and that he has given humanity a life and a home as part of his creation. God is therefore to be blessed for what he has done.

So far I have assumed that the psalmist who wrote Psalm 103 is writing about his own personal experiences of forgiveness, or healing, or of the help and love of God filling his life in some way or another.

It is impossible to say if the psalmist had particular events or moments of his life in mind, or whether he was generalizing about his life history as a whole: but I have assumed that personal experiences lie behind these verses, and that in them the psalmist is giving a personal testimony to God's generosity. There is, however, another possibility; that these verses are not referring to the psalmist's personal experiences at all, but that they are talking about the experience of the community, of the forgiveness of the nation of Israel, or the restoration of the people to their own land, or the renewal of peace and prosperity in the nation. It is the sickness of the nation that has been healed, Israel which has been saved from death and forgiven, and God's people who have been crowned with his love and mercy. One particular suggestion is that this psalm celebrates the return of the people from exile in Babylon around 540 BC, together with the rebuilding of Jerusalem and the resurrection of the nation. That is the setting of Isaiah of Babylon's promise in Isaiah 40, and that chapter has a lot in common with this psalm. Both picture God as a king enthroned above the earth (Isaiah 40.12-23, 25-26, 28 and Psalm 103.19-20); both say that human life is 'like grass' (Isaiah 40.6-8 and 24 and Psalm 103.15), and both use the metaphor of the 'eagle' (Isaiah 40.29-31 and Psalm 103.5). It is possible that the prophet is weaving words and ideas from the older hymn which he had sung into his promises to the exiles in Babylon. It is equally possible that the psalmist is using some of the prophet's words of promise in the new hymn that he is composing to celebrate the return home. Having said all that, they may have nothing to do with each other, for we do not know when, where or by whom Psalm 103 was composed. Its heading – 'Of David' – does not mean that David wrote it, but that this psalm belonged to the Royal Collection in the Temple.

One thing is certain, however, and it is that Psalm 103.2-5 became, whatever the original author may have written or intended, part of a hymn which was and is used in public worship. If verses 2-5 are about the psalmist's personal experience, then his personal praise in these verses was taken up and used by the worshipping community of Israel. The psalmist's very personal testimony was valued and used by others and this must have been because it struck chords with their personal experience of God's love. Or if these verses are about God's deliverance of the people from exile and their restoration in their own land, then the community began to use them not only to celebrate that deliverance, but also to sing God's praises for all the other ways in which he had delivered them through their long history before and after it. Psalm 103 became popular and was then included in the Official Hymn Book, and so these verses became a vehicle for others to use in worship, saying what they wanted and needed to say, so that the psalmist's words took on ever new meanings. When this hymn was and is used in public worship the psalmist's own experience, the personal experience of each singer and the experience of the community blend together. The psalmist gives the words, the congregation fills them with their own meanings: but the two join together in blessing a generous God for his 'benefits'.

All that is well and good, but somebody might object at this point. What happens when people have not been satisfied with good as long as they live? Or when their strength and vitality is far from that of a soaring eagle? What happens when the experience of a community has been invasion or oppression, chaos or disintegration, poverty or ruin? What do those people say whose lives have not been full of steadfast love and mercy, or who have known the pain of life and the absence of God? How are they to sing this psalm? And what are they to think about this allegedly generous God, or the meaning of life? They might say that it's all very well thanking God for flowers and holidays and sunshine, or for good health and friends and little happy babies: but what about all the tragedies of life, the disasters, the starvation, the inhumanity, the disease, suffering and death which have been and still are the experience of most people on our little planet? They might suggest that these terrible realities make the psalmist's gratitude seem a mockery. And they might go on to say that it just shows that he must have been living in a very cosy and self-centred little world, or that 'The writer is too comfortably situated to think or feel deeply' as a commentator said a hundred years ago.

There is certainly strength in this objection, and it can be raised also about the very trivial and self-centred prayers of thanksgiving which we sometimes hear in our church services. But it is not the whole truth, either for the psalmist or for us today. We do indeed live in a world where terrible things happen to people, but so did the psalmist. Life in his world has been described as 'nasty, brutish and short'. Yet in the middle of all the troubles he would without any doubt have experienced, he still finds a voice to praise God. There are many laments among the psalms which focus on life's agonies, and make urgent appeals to God for his help and deliverance: but the Book of Psalms has a place for hymns of praise as well. It is not really fair to dismiss Psalm 103 as a 'fair-weather psalm' at all. It is not a psalm that is just for those for whom life is good and bright and happy. It is a psalm which is well aware of the other side of life which, with full knowledge of the shadows, insists that in the end God is there, reliable and to be trusted. It expresses a faith that the author does not necessarily see working out in practice, that in the end God's will will be done and his justice, love and kindness will be seen. This psalmist, who knows nothing of any life beyond death, and who knows about the difficulties of life this side of it, is yet prepared to praise God for the love that he has shown in the creation of the world, in the gift of life, and in all the varied circumstances of his own life. So another Victorian commentator can say that this psalm was 'composed with a pathos that evidences a soul tried by real sin, sorrow and suffering'.

Whichever of these old commentators you prefer, there is no denying that the opening verses of Psalm 103 picture a generous God. And neither can it be said that this is the only place in the Old Testament where such a picture is painted. These verses might not give the whole picture of what the Old Testament says about God or about the meaning of life, but they make a powerful, positive and life-affirming start.

Questions for reflection

1. Was 'generous' in the list of words describing the God of the Old Testament you made at the end of the Introduction? If not, would you include it now?

2. 'Judaism celebrates life as a gift; Christianity has often seen it as a trial and a temptation' – what do you think about this quotation? In the light of the opening verses of Psalm 103, do you think we celebrate God's 'benefits' enough? If not, how might we do it better?

3. Deuteronomy puts it very simply – 'goodness is rewarded and badness is punished'. What do you think about that bald statement? What do you think are its weaknesses, and its strengths?

4. Psalm 103 insists that God is for us, not against us. Do you agree?

2

A God of steadfast love and mercy

Having looked at the generosity of God in the opening verses of Psalm 103, we now come to one of the most important Old Testament words of all – *chesed* – 'steadfast love' – found four times in our psalm.

> The LORD is the one who crowns you with
> steadfast love and mercy. (Psalm 103.4b)

God does not simply save from death and restore to life, he gives abundant life, full and rich, so that the restored person is like a king or queen, 'crowned' with God's goodness. In this bold image God the king (v. 19) crowns the psalmist!

This metaphor of humans being 'crowned' by God is also found in Psalm 8, which celebrates the majesty and glory of God and the special place he has given to the human race. Compared to the heavens which are the work of God's 'fingers' (not even his hands), mortals are utterly insignificant, yet amazingly God has given them a place in the scheme of things second only to his own, and he has 'crowned them with glory and honour' (Psalm 8.5). Human beings have been made the kings and queens of creation by the God who created them. Great and wonderful gifts have been given to them, and they occupy a privileged place in creation. They have been given 'dominion' over all the animals and over everything else that God has made (Psalm 8.6). This is exactly what is said in the story of creation in Genesis 1.26-31, where the act of creating human beings is the last thing God does before he rests. Humans will have a position of great responsibility, and God trusts them to act responsibly as his agents in the created world. This is what is meant by the saying that men and women are made 'in the image of God' (Genesis 1.26-27), that God has created them to continue his work of creation in guiding and shaping the ongoing life of the world. This is the honour and privilege with which human beings are 'crowned' in Psalm 8.

But as we have already seen, there is no denying that humanity has abused the trust that God has placed in it, and that we have been poor stewards of creation, exploiting and spoiling what was ours to cherish and develop. The psalmist in Psalm 103 has already admitted his 'iniquity', and shown that he is aware that he is far from the person that God intended him to be. No doubt we all have to confess to a 'green' God that we have failed him often, that we have misruled the world instead of taking the opportunity which he gave us to rule it properly. Yet the psalmist knows that after all his failure God has 'crowned' him, not only forgiven and restored him but blessed him with good things, encouraged and enabled him to set his failures aside and to start again, and given back to him his royal place. So the psalmist praises God for 'crowning' him with 'steadfast love and mercy'. He stands amazed at God's generosity.

'Steadfast love' is represented by the wonderfully warm and rich Hebrew word *chesed*. The wealth of meaning in this evocative word can be seen in the variety of ways it has been translated in our Bibles over the years: 'mercy', 'kindness', 'loving-kindness', 'covenant devotion', 'loyalty', 'tenderness', 'faithful love', 'constant love' or just that overworked but basic 'love'. There is a lot to be said for 'steadfast love', for this captures an important aspect of God's love in terms of his covenant with Israel. God calls Israel to be his people, and pledges his loyalty and love to them in the covenant with Moses on Mount Sinai (Exodus 20–24, Deuteronomy 5). In response the people commit themselves to honour God and obey him in all that they do. The ongoing story tells of God's reliability; he keeps his promises and honours his covenant, no matter how unreliable Israel turns out to be. He stays with his people, no matter how often they desert him. His love is reliable, which comes over in the translations '*steadfast* love', '*constant* love' and '*faithful* love'. So the psalmist wants to honour, thank and praise God because he has experienced for himself the same continually faithful and loyal kindness, care and love which God has consistently shown towards the people of Israel. He testifies that God's feelings towards us are both lovingly warm and consistently reliable: unfortunately, as much of the Old Testament so frequently complains, ours towards him are often neither.

Chesed is a rich technical term from the theological vocabulary of the Old Testament, but the other key word in this verse (in the plural, actually, though translated in the singular as 'mercy') is not technical at all. It is an equally warm word but an everyday one. It is a word for the love of parents towards their children, for family love or love between friends, an ordinary word for kindness or compassion, for affection and tenderness, especially towards the weak or those in need. It too is found later in Psalm 103 at verse 8 and twice in verse 13, where it is used of the love a father has for his children. It speaks of the warmth of the affection in which God has held his people, and which the psalmist has known.

Verse 8 begins with the resounding affirmation, 'The LORD is merciful and gracious', which picks up the mention of 'mercy' from verse 4, and adds another blessing to it; and then parallels this powerful declaration of God's love with a restatement of it that mentions his 'anger' before closing with the other term from verse 4, the mighty 'steadfast love' word itself. The second half of verse 8 makes a contrast between God's anger, which is 'slow', and his steadfast love, which 'abounds' and verse 9 takes up the issue of God's anger, though only to say how short-lived it is. This one verse is then followed by three which emphasize the huge extent of his steadfast love. It is as if the four words or phrases of verse 8 are each given a commentary of their own in the four verses that follow, though the only word from verse 8 which reappears is 'steadfast love' in verse 11.

Many commentators call verse 8 a 'confessional formula', for it seems to be something of a mini-creed which crops up in various places in the Old Testament, and it also appears in one of the new psalms found in the Dead Sea Scrolls. The wording varies slightly from place to place, and in some it is longer than others. The four points made in Psalm 103.8 are found in the same order at Psalm 86.15 and Exodus 34.6, though both of these add extra points. The order of the first two words is changed at Psalm 145.8, Joel 2.13 and Jonah 4.2, and each adds an extra point. Other versions, longer and shorter, occur at Numbers 14.18, Nehemiah 9.17, Nahum 1.3, Psalm 111.4 and 2 Chronicles 30.9. These verses come from different strands of Old Testament literature and thought, and from writings which are, as far as we can tell, from very different periods. We can probably conclude from this that this mini-creed said something important about God which was believed by most Israelites. If an ancient Israelite was asked, 'What is your God like?' then the chances are that he or she would point to the Exodus, as we shall see, and say, 'That is what he is like, a God who sets us free.' If they were pressed further it looks as if they might well have gone on to say, 'The LORD is merciful and gracious, slow to anger and abounding in steadfast love.' In fact the two go together. In Psalm 103 this statement of faith in verse 8 immediately follows a reference to the Exodus in verses 6-7, and in most of the 11 places where this mini-creed is found the same is true. This verse seems to be very near to the heart of what they understood about their God.

The close connection between this mini-creed and the Exodus is seen in Exodus 34, where what is probably the oldest of these statements appears. Exodus 34 is another version of the giving of the Law to Moses on Mount Sinai after they had escaped from Egypt. In the story, when Moses had returned from meeting God on Mount Sinai the first time, he found that the people had melted down their gold jewellery and were worshipping a golden calf. He pleaded with God to forgive them, but then set about punishing them himself. In Exodus 34 Moses is back on Mount Sinai again, and is given two new tablets of stone with God's law written on them to replace the original ones which he had thrown down in sorrow or anger at the people's folly. Then we read:

> The LORD descended in the cloud, and stood with him there, and proclaimed the name, 'The LORD.' The LORD passed before him, and proclaimed, 'The LORD, the LORD, a God merciful and gracious, slow to anger, and abounding in steadfast love and faithfulness, keeping steadfast love for the thousandth generation, forgiving iniquity and transgression and sin, yet by no means clearing the guilty, but visiting the iniquity of the parents upon the children, and the children's children to the third and fourth generation.' (Exodus 34.5-7)

The first verse of this is difficult to follow, but 'proclaiming the name of the LORD' and the double repetition of God's special name, 'The LORD', at the beginning of verse 6 clearly show the important connection between this mysterious name and the Exodus. For Israel the LORD is to be their God, he and no other. This verse has all the solemn feel of an old saying used over centuries in public worship. It is strange and awesome. We warm to God's goodness and love in the first phrase, but when we read on these good attributes are eclipsed by what follows. We read of a God who '[visits] the iniquity of the parents on the children and the children's children, to the third and fourth generation' and this is not a God we warm to. All our stereotypes about the nasty God of the Old Testament come into play, and we shall have to face up to them, but here we should note carefully that this old saying puts God's 'anger' in perspective. His punishment might last for three or four generations, but his 'blessing' lasts for a thousand generations! The same point is made in the middle of the Ten Commandments in Exodus 20.5-6, and in a slightly different way in Psalm 30.5:

> For his anger is but for a moment: his
> favour is for a lifetime.
> Weeping may linger for the night, but joy
> comes with the morning.

The other word for God's generous kindness in Psalm 103.8 is 'gracious', another everyday word for human beings being considerate, generous and compassionate to others, especially to people in need. It is not that the psalmist is talking about three different aspects of God's loving character here, rather he is piling up words which all add up to the same thing, a statement of the outstanding and amazing love of God.

The third phrase – 'slow to anger' – is a literal translation of the Hebrew, which might or might not mean that he is 'long-suffering', or 'patient' as some translations put it. If we do choose to say that God is patient, then we need to remember that there are limits to his patience. If we prefer to say that he is 'slow to anger', then we need to note that he does get angry eventually. The reference here to God's anger is important. For all of his love and care expressed in the other words in this verse, God can become angry and we must return to that idea later in this chapter.

> For as the heavens are high above the
>   earth,
> so great is his steadfast love toward those
>   who fear him;
> as far as the east is from the west,
> so far he removes our transgressions
>   from us. (Psalm 103.11-12)

This next appearance of *chesed* stresses the extent of the generosity of God's grace, using words that often speak of the exalted power and glory of God. That God behaves towards human beings in this unbelievably generous way, for there is no way that any human leader would behave like this, is a sign of his true greatness. Using the metaphor of height, the LORD's steadfast love is said to be as 'great' or 'mighty' towards us as the sky or the heavens are 'high' over the earth. The sky stretches above us from one end of the earth to the other; so too the steadfast love of God has no limits. As high as the sky, so God's steadfast love towers over us. Isaiah of Jerusalem often uses metaphors of height to talk about God, saying that God is 'high and lifted up', as in his vision of God enthroned in or above the Temple (Isaiah 6): but when he sees God like this he is made to realize how small and insignificant he is by comparison. Likewise when Ezekiel sees the glory of God and the splendour and marvel of God's power in a vision (Ezekiel 1–3) he too is made to feel insignificant and frightened. But here in the psalm this metaphor of height is not used of God towering in majestic splendour and royal power above us. Nor is it used to suggest a distance between God and us. It is used to illustrate the marvellous extent of God's love, as it is experienced by 'those who fear him'. Then in verse 12 we have the metaphor of distance, to say how far away God has put our 'transgressions' from us. To put something at a distance is to put it out of sight and forget it. So instead of focusing his attention on our sin, and making us do the same, God has thrown it as far away as possible, out of our sight entirely. It ceases to exist as far as we are concerned. God not only distances our sin from us, but he makes that distance as great as possible, 'as far as east is from west' or, possibly, as far as sunrise is from sunset. This indeed is forgiving and forgetting. This is wiping the slate clean and throwing the duster away.

In verse 13 the picture changes from the world of nature to the everyday world of human relationships, and pictures God behaving towards us as a father does towards his children. Great distances and far horizons are one way of expressing God's love and generosity, the intimacy of family life is another:

> As a father has compassion for his children,
> so the LORD has compassion for those who fear him.

The picture of God as a father is not very prominent in the Old Testament, but it is there. We have already seen how important the idea of God as the saviour of his people is in the Old Testament, and another significant theme is that God is the creator of the world. In places both of these ideas are linked with the picture of God as father. In Deuteronomy 32.6, which is part of a sermon which the writer has put on the lips of Moses, the congregation is accused of forsaking God and Moses turns on them with the question:

> 'Do you thus repay the LORD, O foolish and senseless people? Is he not your father, who created you, who made you and established you?'

Earlier in the sermon the people of Israel were reminded that they are God's 'children':

> You are the children of the LORD your God … you are a people holy to the LORD your God; it is you the LORD has chosen out of all the peoples on earth to be his people, his treasured possession.
> (Deuteronomy 14.1-2)

In the Exodus story the people of Israel are called God's 'son' when Moses is instructed to go to Pharaoh and say, 'Thus says the LORD, "Israel is my firstborn son … let my son go that he may worship me." ' (Exodus 4.22-23, see also Hosea 11.1).

After the people have been settled in Israel for hundreds of years Isaiah of Jerusalem expresses God's sorrow for the rebellious way that his children have behaved (Isaiah 1.2-3). Later in Isaiah this picture of God as father is combined with that of God as a potter:

> Yet, O LORD, you are our Father, we are the clay, and you are our potter; we are all the work of your hand' and '… you are our father … you, O LORD, are our father, our Redeemer from of old is your name (Isaiah 64.8 and 63.16).

31

Jeremiah sees God as a father reuniting his scattered children, bringing the exiles of the old Northern Kingdom back to join his children in Judah (Jeremiah 31.9). But the result bitterly disappoints him for they misbehave as before: 'And I thought you would call me, My Father, and would not turn from following me' (Jeremiah 3.19).

Nowhere in the Old Testament is this picture of God's parental care for the children of Israel and their rejection of such love more beautifully and poignantly put than in Hosea 11.1-4:

> When Israel was a child I loved him ... it
> was I who taught Ephraim to walk, I took
> them up in my arms ... I led them with
> cords of human kindness ... I was to them
> like those who lift infants to their cheeks.
> I bent down to them and fed them.

Hosea says sharply that although God had loved them so much – and here the picture is of God as a mother – they had insisted on going their own way.

There is one other area in the thought of the Old Testament where the picture of God as Father is very clear and important. God is seen as the father of the king in Jerusalem, and the king of David's line is seen as the Son of God. So in the early days of the monarchy the prophet Nathan goes to King David and promises that David will have a son who will build the Temple that David dearly wanted to build, and that God will bless this son: 'I will be a father to him, and he shall be a son to me' (2 Samuel 7.14, see also 1 Chronicles 28.6). And in the Coronation service the newly anointed king testifies: 'I will tell of the decree of the LORD: He said to me, "You are my son; today I have begotten you" ' (Psalm 2.7). So it is that the king, God's 'firstborn', can cry out to God: 'You are my Father, my God, and the Rock of my salvation!' (Psalm 89.26-27).

Twice in the Psalter other people than the king are encouraged to see God and his care in this way. God is called the 'father of orphans and protector of widows' (Psalm 68.5), and another psalmist can say, 'If my father and mother forsake me, the LORD will take me up' (Psalm 27.10).

From all of this we can see that the metaphor of God as father is a rich one. It blends images taken from family life of the father as the head of the family, master of the household, authority figure and disciplinarian, provider and protector, lover, begetter of children and one who cares for them and loves them, with images of the king as father of the people, their protector and the source of their vitality, energy and prosperity. To say that God is father is to speak of him as maker of the world and its life-giver, as protector of the people of Israel and their master, and as the one who loves those he calls his children. The use of the metaphor in Psalm 103 focuses on the last of these ideas. As a father God 'has compassion for his children'. Here, therefore, we have a wonderfully warm metaphor of God as a father caring for and loving his children. When God's children do wrong, as the psalmist knows very well that they do, he does not throw them out of the house, or nurse his anger indefinitely, but can be relied on to treat them as a loving father would. This is the clue to understanding God's 'anger' in the Bible.

The Old Testament and the New both agree that God exhibits anger and that this anger is directed against evil and at human sin. The psalmist is aware of the shadow side of human life, and the Old Testament is fully aware of how damaging 'iniquity', 'sin' and 'wickedness' can be. It is not something to be treated lightly or dismissed easily. Sin, in all its chameleon colours, makes God angry because it fouls up his creation and spoils life for its victims. And, surely, in the face of this it would be a poor God who did not get angry? The God of the Bible gets angry when he sees what has happened to his creation, for 'he has made nothing in vain and loves all that he has made'. Only a heartless and unloving God would not. A God who did not get angry would be as useless and as uncaring as a parent who did not care how badly one of their children hurt the others, or how much damage they did to themselves or other people. The picture of a parent is important here, for good parents do get angry, and they get angry because they care. Here the psalmist voices the common view of his faith that God feels anger, just as we do, with all its potent mixture of rage, grief, frustration, hurt and fear, and he does so because he cares. God's anger, then, is not a contradiction of his love, but a sign of it. The psalmist believes in the reality of God's anger, and is deeply grateful that the LORD is 'slow to anger' and that his anger has limits. He is grateful that God will not go on accusing or being angry if he turns from those wicked ways which made him angry in the first place. He knows this both from his own experience of God's forgiveness (v. 3) and what he has seen in Israel's history.

As the metaphor of God's anger can cause problems, so can that of God as father. It is often pointed out that many people have not had good experiences of human fathers. In addition there is a growing number of both Jews and Christians, women and men, who find it impossible to talk of God as 'Father' because a 'father', obviously, is a male, and God is not male. The question of whether or not to carry on using the metaphor of 'father' for God or what to put in place of calling God 'Father' is a difficult one. Psalm 103 uses masculine pronouns for God because Hebrew is just like English in this respect, but verse 13 is quite clear on the wider point – God loves 'those who fear him' in the same way as parents love their children. The psalm uses the picture of a caring father as an illustration of how God cares, and to change the word 'father' to 'parent' or 'parents' in the verse would not detract from the point of the metaphor at all. The picture would be just as vivid and powerful. Those who never knew their parents or whose experiences of being parented have not been pleasant would still have problems, but the great advantage would be that the psalm no longer gave the impression that God was male.

The last reference to *chesed* comes in verses 15-18, which are printed as a distinct section in the NRSV and most modern versions. In many ways, however, verses 15-16 follow very closely on verse 14 and continue to illustrate the theme of human frailty in that verse:

> As for mortals, their days are like grass;
>   they flourish like a flower of the field;
> for the wind passes over it, and it is gone,
>   and its place knows it no more.
> But the steadfast love of the LORD
>   is from everlasting to everlasting
>   on those who fear him,
>   and his righteousness to children's
>   children,
> to those who keep his covenant
>   and remember to do his commandments.

As human beings are made of the dust of the ground, so their lives are as short as the grass or the flowers which grow out of the same ground. As the dust blows away and leaves little or no trace, so when the hot summer wind has finished blowing over the fields there is little or nothing left where the grass and flowers have been. How different it is with God's steadfast love (vv. 17-18). His *chesed* lasts for ever, spreading its shade like a huge old tree over the generations as they come and go. For us, of course, grass is permanent! This reminds us that the Bible originated in a place where the geography is different from ours.

Verse 17 has a strong claim to be the crescendo of the psalm. Pictures of the transience of human life – dust, quickly fading grass and flowers, and wind which blows and is gone – are replaced in this verse with statements of the durability and continuity of the LORD's steadfast love. The immortality of God's constant work to put things right (his 'righteousness') is contrasted with our mortality. The infinity of God's love is 'from everlasting to everlasting'; it stretches 'to children's children', to the 'thousandth generation'.

'From everlasting to everlasting' is translated as 'for ever' in some of the modern versions. This is not strong enough and fails to catch the power of the word 'everlasting'. Isaiah of Babylon sees Cyrus the Persian advancing on Babylon and the end of their exile is in sight:

> So the ransomed of the LORD shall return, and come to Zion with singing; everlasting joy shall be upon their heads; they shall obtain joy and gladness, and sorrow and sighing shall flee away. (Isaiah 51.11)

Of course they will rejoice and be glad, who wouldn't in their circumstances? But Isaiah is saying that their joy is far deeper than that. It is 'everlasting' joy, because they will be sharing in the same sort of experience of God's power that the 'generations of long ago' experienced (v. 9 – literally 'the everlasting generations') at the creation of the world and at the deliverance from Egypt, for these events are what

Isaiah has in mind in these verses. In that moment, brief and passing though inevitably it will be, they will be in touch with something ultimate, with what is real. They will experience the great creative force which is behind the universe. So the Old Testament talks of the 'everlasting hills', the 'everlasting doors' of the Temple and the 'everlasting covenant' of God with his people, not only because these things will last for ever but also because they are especially filled with the mystery and power of the cosmic God's eternity. This is put beautifully in the old translations of Deuteronomy 33.27:

> The eternal God is your dwelling place,
> and underneath are the everlasting arms.

Of course God's arms last for ever, and are around us for all time: but by using the word 'everlasting' this verse invites us to feel the strength of God's arms, to feel secure in their grip, to take comfort in their warmth, and to be reassured by the way they hold us up. These are God's arms and there is nothing to fear, for he is creator of the world and its mighty saviour. He is the cosmic Lord, beyond time and beyond all creation. All of that comes over in the word 'everlasting'. So when Psalm 103.17 says that 'the steadfast love of the LORD is from everlasting to everlasting on those who fear him', those who sing the psalm are not only reminded that God's love lasts for ever, but they are also invited to feel the strength of this mighty love around them and upon them, that they are eternally valued by the king of creation, 'eternally held in (God's) heart'.

The second picture in verse 17 is much more homely. God is like a grandparent! It was one of life's crowning joys to live to see one's grandchildren (Psalm 128.6; Proverbs 17.6). In verse 17 the psalmist uses this picture. The LORD feels the same joy over us as grandparents feel over their grandchildren. As grandparents delight in grandchildren so God delights in us. As grandparents try to do their best for their grandchildren so that all may go well with them as they start out in life, so God does his best for us. He works to put things right and keep them right for us so that we might live life to the full, for that is what the psalm means when it says that God's 'righteousness' is 'to' us, as we shall see in our discussion of 'righteousness' in the next chapter.

We came across the expression 'to children's children' in Exodus 34.7 where it was part of a solemn warning that sin can spoil human life, and that its punishment and its damaging effects can spread down the generations even to great-grandchildren. We also noted, however, that in those verses this punishment is very limited when compared with the scope of God's forgiveness and his blessing. In Psalm 103.17 no limit is put on God's desire and work to put things right. God puts things right 'to children's children' on and on through the generations. In verses 11-12 the psalm used the dimensions of height and breadth to describe God's steadfast love, it is as high as the sky and as wide as the world. Verse 17 now adds the other dimensions of time and space to that picture. It is as enduring as the time-span from before creation to after the end of the world, and as real as this world and the one beyond it. It has no more limits than the limits of grandparents' love for their grandchildren.

Questions for reflection

1. Has anything surprised you in this exploration of the 'steadfast love' of God in the Old Testament?

2. What do you think are the strengths and weaknesses of thinking of God as a 'loving father'?

3. 'Love can be sentimental or it can be tough – but it can't be both – and God's steadfast love is the tough sort.' What do you think?

4. What do you think about God's anger? Is it a sign that he cares? Or have I played down the vengeful side of the Old Testament God?

3

A God of justice and righteousness

After the very personal introduction in which the psalmist calls on everything in him to praise the LORD, the psalm moves in verses 6-14 into a more public area, setting out what the LORD has done for the nation of Israel (vv. 6-7) and for 'those who fear him' (vv. 10-14). The 'steadfast love' and 'mercy' which the psalmist has experienced in his own life (v. 4) has also been God's attitude to the nation as a whole (v. 8). As the psalmist feels that he had been treated like royalty so he is equally grateful that God has so generously blessed all those who have looked for his help (vv. 11-13). So the psalm now calls on each worshipper to recognize that the LORD is to be praised for what he has done for Israel, and for all 'those who fear him' (vv. 6, 8 and 13). Here is wider testimony to what God is like. He can be seen in what he has done. This central part of the hymn opens with two verses (6-7) which introduce us to two more key, but much misunderstood, words:

> The LORD works vindication
>   and justice for all who are oppressed.
> He made known his ways to Moses,
>   his acts to the people of Israel.

Here we see the belief that the LORD has acted on behalf of his people, saving them from their enemies and giving them victory in their battles, giving the oppressed victory over their oppressors. In a way there is nothing unusual in this, for it was a common idea in the ancient Near East that the gods operated in history. Everyone agreed that your national god or gods brought you prosperity in your harvests and victory in your wars, or their opposites, and Israel shared this way of thinking. So they told their stories of how the LORD their God had blessed them, or of how he had punished them. The great events of their history, especially the Exodus but also their occupation of their Promised Land, the capture of Jerusalem, and the expansion and prosperity of the kingdom under David and Solomon, were all due to the LORD their God, acting on their behalf. And they explained their defeats, famines and the terrible events of the fall of Jerusalem and the exile in the same way; these were the work of the LORD, acting in these dreadful ways to punish them for their sins. The action of God in the world of current affairs, international politics, the rise and fall of nations or kings in war and battle, and in economic success or failure can be seen in the Old Testament almost anywhere in the books from Deuteronomy to 2 Kings.

The greatest example of God's saving acts for his people, as far as the Old Testament is concerned, is his deliverance of the Israelites from slavery in Egypt. The LORD heard their cry and saved them under the leadership of Moses, bringing them out of Egypt in the Exodus. Psalm 105, for example, tells of 'all the LORD's wonderful works' beginning with his promises to Abraham, but the core of the psalm is about the Exodus from Egypt and the entry into the Promised Land. So in Psalm 103 the general statement that God saves the oppressed in verse 6 is immediately followed by the reference to the Exodus in verse 7. As we saw, if it were possible to ask a group of ancient Israelites about their belief in God, they would be supposed to answer – 'If you want to know what God is like, and who the LORD is whom we worship, then remember the Exodus!' The storytellers among them would also point out, however, that there is another side to that story. Not only is the Exodus the great example of God at work to save his people, it is also a good example of his people's ingratitude and stubborn resistance to him. It is a tale of their grumbling against Moses and against God, of wanting to go back to the relative comforts of Egypt, and of turning to other gods as soon as Moses' back was turned; of 'grace abounding and benefits forgot'.

> The LORD works vindication and justice
> for all who are oppressed. (v. 6)

This verse begins in the same way as the items in the psalmist's personal list, the LORD 'is the one who ...', and gives us two more 'benefits' which the LORD has given to Israel. It makes three points: first, that the LORD is a God who acts, who does something; second, that he acts for or in 'vindication' (righteousness) and 'justice'; and, third, that he does what he does for the 'oppressed'.

A God who acts

The idea that God acts in history has passed into Christian thinking, and Christians have traditionally believed that God was acting in the world in the life of Jesus, in special ways in his miracles and throughout his life; and also guiding and shaping events in general with a plan in mind. The cross and resurrection were the work of God; he caused the crucifixion to take place, and he raised Jesus from the dead. God was at work in these mighty acts, and continued to be at work in building the Church and making it spread throughout the world. Some Christians have gone so far as to believe that nothing at all happens without God being at work; that he has planned everything, and life unfolds according to his planning. Most Christians do not accept that our lives are predetermined and planned in this way, or accept the ideas of predestination which often go with this view, but it is not only insurance companies which talk about 'acts of God'. Ordinary Christians will give thanks to God for what he has done for them, or will pray for him to act for their benefit in one way or another, though they recognize that God's arm cannot be twisted, and that they must have the humility to ask in a spirit of 'your will, not mine, be done'. Churches share the same view, and thanksgiving services are held on all kinds of occasions to give thanks to God for what he has done. He has been involved. He has acted. He has changed things. The psalmist said much the same. He believed, as most people in his part of the ancient world believed, that God could do things.

There are, however, huge and unavoidable difficulties in this way of thinking; and they can be seen very clearly if we use the example of healing. In Psalm 103.3 the psalmist spoke about God acting to heal him, and prayers for healing then and now are offered in the belief that God can and does heal. But we know that not all prayers for healing result in healing, and if we ask why they do not, we find that two sorts of answers are usually given. One suggests that the answer lies with us, often along the lines that the person who prayed did not have enough faith or the right kind of faith and so on. The other suggests that the answer lies with God, that he knows best and for some reason chose not to act this time. If we ask why God should choose not to do anything in a particular case, we usually get the reply that God answers prayers for healing in three ways: yes, no or not yet. In many Christian circles it would be considered a lack of faith, if not heresy, to say that God didn't answer this or that prayer for healing for the simple reason that he couldn't. Such is the grip that the idea of a God who acts in the world has on our understanding. Indeed, many would say that a God who doesn't act is no God at all, that a God who does not play an active role in the world is a dead

God, and simply conclude, 'If God can't do anything about it, why should I bother to pray or to believe in him at all?'

Exploring this question much further would take us too far out of the Old Testament, but two things can be said here. The first is that we have already seen that the writer of Psalm 103 knew about illness and suffering, and we can also say for certain that he had sung those psalms of lament which cry out to a God who seems absent or helpless (e.g. Psalms 38, 44 and 74) and which the Old Testament is bold enough to include in its pages. He knew, therefore, that this was a real question. The second is that in Psalm 103 the psalmist qualifies the general statement that God does things, by saying what he does and for whom, and by hinting about how he acts. That hint is found in the mention of Moses, and it might give us a clue to help us in some of our difficulties about thinking of a 'God who acts' and how God 'works' in the world of human history. The Old Testament talks about the Exodus as a mighty act of God:

> The LORD brought us out of Egypt with a
> mighty hand and an outstretched arm,
> with a terrifying display of power, and
> with signs and wonders ...
> (Deuteronomy 26.8)

And it is true that all through the stories in Exodus, Leviticus and Numbers there are miracles large and small, nice and nasty, from the parting of the waters of the Sea of Reeds, through the daily gift of the manna to eat, to the causing of earthquakes to swallow those who grumbled at Moses. But for all of these demonstrations of his power it is absolutely basic to the story that God called Moses and that, with Aaron and Miriam, Moses negotiated with Pharaoh and led the people out of Egypt and through the desert, and that on Mount Sinai God made the covenant with and through Moses. Even the waters of the sea did not part until Moses raised his staff and held out his arm over them (Exodus 14.21). Crucial roles in the drama were played by human actors, especially the all-too-human Moses. God did not simply appear to the Israelites and lead them out of Egypt. He used Moses as his agent, just as he used him as the go-between to set up the covenant on Mount Sinai. Telling the story in this way suggests that God *needed* Moses, or somebody, to make it all possible. He did not do it all by himself, because he couldn't. He could only do this work through a human agent, so God called Moses and used Moses. The key role of Moses is an undeniable part of the Exodus story. There is much truth in the words of this prayer attributed to St Teresa and of the old Sunday school ditty, provided we take out the word 'Christ' and put in the word 'God':

> Christ has no body now on earth but yours;
> no hands but yours, no feet but yours.
> Yours are the eyes through which must look out
> Christ's compassion on the world.
> Yours are the feet with which he is to go about doing good.
> Yours are the hands with which he is to bless men now.

> Christ has no hands but our hands
> to do his work today.

This might not be all that should be said about how God acts in history, but it is an essential part of the discussion. The Old Testament tells story after story of how God calls, equips, guides and encourages people to see his purposes and to share in working them out. These may be great tasks or small, and the people in them range from the likely to the unlikely, from the religious professional to the total amateur, and from the great and powerful to the small and seemingly insignificant. Some he uses only once, while for others the commitment is for life, and the long list in Hebrews 11 of those who had 'faith', heard the call of God in one way or another and responded to it so that God's work could be done is a fascinating read.

Righteousness/vindication (*tsedaqah*)

The second point made in verse 6 is about the way God works, that he acts for or in 'vindication' and 'justice', and these are two important and much misunderstood Old Testament technical terms. There are two minor complications here to begin with: the first is that the NRSV translates the Hebrew term as 'vindication' rather than 'righteousness' and the second is that in this verse both words are in the plural, and translating them literally as 'righteousnesses' and 'justices' is impossible. The real problem, however, is that in Christian teaching these two terms have taken on quite different meanings from those in the Old Testament and probably also in the New. The result is that we tend to read both the New Testament and the Old wrongly when we read these words. Finding a modern English equivalent for 'righteousness' which conveys the real sense of the Hebrew is very difficult, and the problem with 'justice' is that Old Testament justice and English justice are not quite the same thing.

Verse 6 celebrates the fact that the LORD puts things right; and 'righteousness' is all to do with being right and putting right.

Weights and measures need to be 'right', so there are rules and regulations in the Old Testament, as in every society, to ensure that weights and measures are accurate. If weights and measures are incorrect then people can be cheated in the market; roofs will not fit on houses if the bricklayer building the walls has a slightly different measuring stick from the carpenter preparing the roof joists. Human beings need to be 'right' for much the same reasons. To function properly their health needs to be right, their attitude needs to be right, and so do their morals. Examples of people who are not right would include those who are sick, selfish, victimized, anti-social, exploited, immoral, sinful or neglected. Some of these are not right because they have done wrong themselves, others are not right because other people have done wrong to them. Personal relationships need to be 'right', with husbands and wives living together in harmony, with honesty and integrity in friendships, and with neighbours getting on with each other. Society needs to be 'right', with law and order, proper provision for the care of the weak and vulnerable, and freedom and encouragement for all to reach their full potential. The nation needs to be 'right', and this means that its borders are safely marked and defended and that there are good relationships with surrounding countries so that all its citizens can live in peace. It will also mean that the nation is faithfully honouring its God, that king and government are 'walking in his ways' so that everyone can enjoy his blessings. As there are rules and regulations for keeping weights and measures right, and for correcting them when they have gone wrong, so there are rules and regulations for almost everything else. 'The laws, the statutes and the ordinances' of the Old Testament are there so that everything can be kept right, or can be put right again when they go wrong. When everything and everybody is 'right' they are living as God intended them to live. He wants harmony, prosperity and peace (*shalom*) for all people, and when that is happening everything is 'right'.

The facts of life, of course, are that the world and its people are not very often 'right' like this. There is 'sin', 'iniquity' and 'evil', as the psalmist said in verse 3. He thanks God for putting him right again when he had gone wrong, restoring him to health and forgiving his sin. That is what God is concerned to do for society and for the world as well as for individuals. It is a mammoth task, and it is this concern and activity to put things right and keep them right which is meant when the Old Testament says that God is 'righteous'. He does this because he loves his creation and wants only the best for it. He hates to see it go wrong and he hates to see the misery caused by people going wrong and doing wrong. The God of 'steadfast love' and 'mercy' wants to 'save' the world and its people from this evil and folly, and 'salvation' is precisely this, it is putting things 'right' again, and keeping them that way. In other places in the Old Testament the plural word found here is translated as 'the *triumphs* of the LORD' (Judges 5.11, about a victory in battle), 'the *saving acts* of the LORD' (Micah 6.5, about events surrounding the Exodus) and 'the *saving deeds* of the LORD' (1 Samuel 12.7, also about the Exodus). The LORD puts things right – he is righteous – and we must imagine the deep sense of joy and celebration which fills the psalmist when he thinks about God's 'righteousness'.

However, the old words 'righteous' and 'righteousness' do not suggest any of this to us, and they do not have a warm or happy feel. When we hear that 'God is righteous', or when someone talks about 'the righteousness of God', if anyone does any more, then we get a quite different impression from that which the psalmist would have had. For him these ideas spoke powerfully about God's loving and generous kindness towards his world, his benevolence which leads him to act to save it. The psalmist knew that at times this meant that God would punish individuals or nations, just as a loving parent has to discipline a misbehaving child. He also knew that this care would involve rules and regulations, and he would have fully understood the need for laws to curb human selfishness and sin, for what the old prayer called 'the restraining of wickedness and vice'. But he would have seen all of this as something positive, that it was all for his good because God was interested in making life as full and rich as possible for him. So when he heard people say that he himself should be 'righteous' and practise 'righteousness' (e.g. Amos 5.24, Proverbs 12.28, Isaiah 5.7) he would have agreed wholeheartedly, for it was something he would have wanted to be and it was a promise about what he could be. It was a call to be right and do right, to be blessed and be a blessing to others, to enjoy and to share in God's fullness of life, his salvation.

It is different for us, because for us 'righteous' and 'righteousness' are cold and hard words. To say that someone is 'self-righteous' is to say something uncomplimentary, and in popular usage 'righteous' and 'self-righteous' amount to much the same thing. This is not a new idea, and it is a sad fact that all religion produces good people who know that they are good and are proud of it, the sort of people who give goodness and religion a bad name. We can see that 'righteous' was getting a bad name even by the time of St Paul by these verses from Romans:

> For while we were still weak, at the right time Christ died for the ungodly. Indeed, rarely will anyone die for a righteous person – though perhaps for a good person someone might actually dare to

die. But God proves his love for us in that while we were still sinners Christ died for us. (Romans 5.6-8)

Paul knows that people feel differently about a 'good' person and a 'righteous' one – no one would sacrifice their life to save a righteous person, though they just might for a good person. So even by Paul's time 'righteous' was becoming an unattractive idea in the minds of some people at least, and it certainly feels like that for us. When we read that God is 'righteous' the impression created is that he is demanding and judgemental. When we read that we are to be 'righteous', the impression is that we are to try very hard to keep all kinds of rules and regulations. All this is a far cry from the meanings of these words in the Old Testament. This unfeeling picture of God is the very opposite of the sense of 'righteous' in the Old Testament.

Justice (*mishpat*)

We can make the same mistake about God's justice or his 'judgement', as older translations used to call it, the other gift for which the psalmist wants to thank God in verse 6. In the singular the Hebrew word for 'justice' can be used for a particular law or a legal ruling, a judgement given by a judge, and so it is translated as 'ordinance' or 'judgement' in many places. It can also be used to mean 'justice' in the abstract. It occurs here paired with 'righteousness' as it often does elsewhere (look again at Isaiah 5.7 and Amos 5.24). Other psalms picture God as the king, who 'judges the world with righteousness' seen (9.8) or unseen (96.13, 97.2, 98.9). The king in Jerusalem is God's anointed son, who needs God's justice and righteousness in order to promote the welfare of the people and protect the poor (Psalm 72.1-2).

These days we hear a lot of talk about justice; it is

one of the 'in' words of the Church. So we nod our approval to a God of justice. But we don't feel the same about a 'God of judgement'. It conjures up pictures of the Last Judgement, of heaven and hell, and of punishment meted out by an angry God. For us 'justice' and 'judgement' are quite different, the one full of positive messages, the other negative. For the Old Testament, however, they are one and the same, and the Old Testament meaning is much more like the positive reaction we give to 'justice'. What, then, does the Old Testament mean by 'justice' and what is it saying when it calls God a 'judge' and says that he 'judges' his people?

In a British courtroom justice is an abstract, impartial norm and the judge must 'impartially and indifferently administer justice' in the quaint phraseology of the *Book of Common Prayer*. The judge does not allow personal feelings to intrude. Everyone has to be treated equally under the law and it is the judge's job to ensure that the scales of justice are evenly balanced. If the accused is found guilty, the punishment must fit the crime, so that the balance of justice is restored. When we apply that idea to God, as we are accustomed to do from the images of the Last Judgement and so on, we see a stern and forbidding figure carefully reckoning up our deeds and our misdeeds. The picture is made worse by talking about Jesus as the one who 'intercedes' for us, pleading for clemency and trying to convince the judge that there are mitigating circumstances. The Bible does talk about God as judge and about Jesus interceding for us, but the picture I have just sketched is not what the Bible means when it talks about judges and justice. We picture it in this way from our western view of justice, which comes ultimately from Roman law, and then apply our ideas to God, with quite dreadful results.

The best way to understand what the Old Testament means by justice, whether it is the justice of God or the justice expected to be seen in personal and social life, is to take a cue from the book of Judges. The 'Judges' after which that book is named were certainly not impartial courtroom administrators or lawyers, though some of them did sometimes preside over village courts and make rulings (e.g. Deborah, Judges 4.4-5). Instead they were freedom fighters raised up and empowered by God's Spirit to deliver his people in times of oppression and crisis, the prophetess Deborah no less than the others. In fact, a better title for that book would be 'The Book of Deliverers' or 'Saviours'. These mighty men, and in one case a mighty woman, were those who saved and delivered God's people from their enemies, restoring the harmony and peace which was God's will for his people. And that, in a nutshell, is what the Old Testament means by justice: the restoration and then the maintenance of harmony and well-being, of righteousness and of peace (*shalom*). Therefore, to say that God is 'just' or to picture him as a 'judge' is to say that he is a saving God, active in seeking, restoring and promoting the total well-being of his people. He is the one who puts his people right. That is 'justice' in its Old Testament sense.

In ancient Israel the courts existed to promote the health of society, restoring its equilibrium by punishing wrongdoing, and providing the opportunity for individuals to have their rights restored when they had been violated. There were simple family 'courts', in that the head of the family or clan was held to be responsible for the behaviour of his family, and had to arbitrate in family disputes. There were local courts, 'in the gate', their equivalent to our town squares or village greens, where the elders met to set things to rights. There were courts of appeal presided over by the local prophet or priest, like Deborah; and, if the situation were more serious, before the king himself. Their rules of evidence, and their sanctions, were different from ours, and there was no real prison system. For justice to be done victims were to be compensated for their losses or injuries, offenders were to be made to see the errors of their ways and to mend them, paying compensation to their victims, and the harmony of society was to be restored so that everyone could play their proper useful role again. We know from frequent references that all this was easily abused and open to corruption, but the system was designed to restore right relationships all round, and it was the primary responsibility of the 'judge' to see that it happened.

The oppressed

In Psalm 103.6 the psalmist celebrates that the LORD is Israel's 'judge', that he is the great example of putting things right and doing justice; a variation on the common theme in the psalms that God 'judges the world with righteousness' (Psalm 9.8). The particular aspect of this that is celebrated here is that God gives back to the 'oppressed' their proper place in life. 'To do justice' or 'to be righteous' is to live in such a way that the well-being of society is promoted, good relationships all round are enhanced, and, very practically, the poor, the needy, the victimized and the abused are cared for; and that is God's duty as well as ours. In the Old Testament there is considerable concern for the vulnerable members of society and many of the psalms see God as the special help of the 'the poor and needy'. They cry out to him in urgent appeal for help (e.g. Psalms 10, 12 and 86), and he comes to their aid (Psalms 9, 20, 27). Special provisions are made in law for 'the widow, the poor, the orphan and the resident alien', a phrase which is used to speak of those who are particularly vulnerable and liable to be exploited or neglected (e.g. Exodus 22.21-24, Deuteronomy 14.29). These people are God's special care (Deuteronomy 10.18-19). He is the 'Father of orphans and protector of widows' (Psalm 68.5). His care and concern for these people is channelled through the king, who is to be the defender of the weak and the friend of the poor as in Psalm 72.1-4, a prayer for the king to receive God's 'justice and righteousness' so that he can carry out God's will:

> Give the king your justice, O God,
>   and your righteousness to a king's son.
> May he judge your people with righteousness,
>   and your poor with justice.
> May the mountains yield prosperity for the people,
>   and the hills, in righteousness.
> May he defend the cause of the poor of the people,
>   give deliverance to the needy,
>   and crush the oppressor.

In Psalm 103.6 the psalmist, at one with prophets like Amos, believes that God cares for the victimized and abused, the exploited and the marginalized, the poor and the weak. He knows that God both demands social justice and works to bring it about. He rejoices that God is 'righteous and just' – two of the most encouraging, reassuring and beautiful words he can use about the God of Israel.

The Exodus

Finally, how does Israel's belief about the Exodus – that greatest example of all of God's active care for the oppressed – square with the facts? According to the story it was a great and dramatic event, involving huge numbers of people, played out on the stage of world history and leaving a terrible legacy of loss and destruction in Egypt. If anything of the history of Israel was going to leave its mark on world history, then one would expect it to be the Exodus. Even if the great kings David and Solomon were hardly noticed outside Israel, one would expect Moses and the Exodus to be mentioned somewhere. In fact, there is no mention of Moses, Israelites, plagues or anything from the story of the Exodus in any of the historical records of the time. Some scholars say that the silence of the Egyptian records on the subject can be explained by the fact that nobody in the ancient world mentioned their defeats anyway, but much more likely is the explanation that the Bible stories themselves make more of the events than was really there. The stories contain all the drama and tension, magic and miracle, exaggerated numbers and divine interventions that characterize lively storytelling and the tendency of all religious reporters to exaggerate. Examined carefully it is impossible to discover the route taken by the fleeing Israelites, or to locate many of the sites mentioned. Some parts of the Old Testament call God's holy mountain Mount Sinai while others call it Mount Horeb, but we have no idea where it was, even if we assume that these are just different names for the same hill. One of the few certainties about the story about Moses' parting of the waters is that they were not those of 'the mighty Red Sea' but of the Sea of Reeds (though few translations use this proper translation of the Hebrew), but where it was no one is certain either. There is no agreement among scholars as to the date of the event or the name of the Pharaoh concerned; we do not have any reliable information about what actually happened. There may have been no more than a few hundred escaping slaves who gave their pursuers the slip by struggling through a windy marsh: but whatever it was, they saw it as a mighty act of God to be celebrated in 'story, song and law'.

The story of the Exodus in the Old Testament is not history in our sense of the word. It is not plain fact. The story does not tell us what actually happened, but when we think about it we know that there is no such thing as 'plain fact', nor any such thing as plain history in any case. Everything that we know from the past we know because somebody told us, one way or another, and all we know is what they told us. They told us what they wanted to tell us. They told us what they thought we ought to know. They told us as they saw it. Someone else who saw it differently would tell it in a different way. There are facts in what we call history, but they are so embedded in interpretation that they can hardly be disentangled. That applies to the Exodus as to everything else. So what we have in the story of the Exodus is testimony. It may have begun when those who had escaped from Egypt told their story, and invited others to join in their way of looking at things, to believe in a God who is on the side of the oppressed and who sets the prisoners free. Those who heard the story could believe it and respond, making it their story too. The testimony was given, not to be believed because its details could be proved, but taken on trust and made the basis for a different way of living. The story was told and retold, and the story lasted because it told of the way things *are* and of how God *is*. A community of faith grew, made up of those who said that this was the story they wanted to live by, and in worship and song through the generations they told the story and handed it on – the story of the righteousness and justice of God, the active saviour of his people.

Questions for reflection

1. What associations did the word 'righteous' and 'righteousness' have for you before you read this chapter? Do you see them differently now?

2. If a Christian preacher tells the congregation that 'you sinners will all stand before the judgement seat of God' – that is a threat and the preacher expects them to be very worried. If a rabbi tells the congregation that 'you sinners will all stand before the judgement seat of God' – that is an encouragement and the rabbi expects them to be very relieved. Does this help you to see the different meaning of 'judge', 'justice' and 'judgement' in the Old Testament?

3. 'A few hundred escaping slaves who gave their pursuers the slip by struggling through a windy marsh.' How do you respond to the suggestion that that is all that the Exodus might have been?

4. 'I find it very difficult to talk about a "God who acts" because he doesn't seem to do it where he really ought to.'

   'If God doesn't act, why should I bother to pray or to believe in him at all?'

   What are the strengths and weaknesses of these opposite points of view? Which one are you more comfortable with?

4

A God of forgiveness

The God of steadfast love, righteousness and justice – for these three terms in their Old Testament meanings add up to pretty much the same thing as we have seen – is a God who forgives, and in verse 3 the psalmist gratefully acknowledges the forgiveness of his own 'iniquity'. And here we see one of humanity's central problems and God's solution to it in a radical nutshell. The English word that is used most in religious circles for this problem is 'sin' and the Bible is full of it. It uses many different words for it, and 'sin' provides one of its main story-lines as well as the theme for many of its stories. A list of words for sin would include: wickedness, evil, wrongdoing, transgression, iniquity, failure, error, vice, trespass and offence. Closely related are words like guilt, crime, immorality and impurity. We can also make lists of actions or attitudes which the Bible calls 'sins', symptoms of the underlying disorder itself, and although these lists may be revised from time to time with new sins added and older ones removed, the reality of which these words speak is as evident today as ever.

One of the better known stories of 'iniquity' in the Old Testament is the sordid story of David's relationship with Bathsheba in 2 Samuel 11–12. Here is sex and violence, deceit and intrigue, and then tragedy that lasts for centuries. David, the great hero king, rapes the beautiful married woman, Bathsheba. Pregnancy follows. David arranges for her absent soldier husband to be killed in battle. The king marries the widow. The baby dies. But that is not the end of the story, for the next child by this woman is

Solomon. David's palace and the whole country is torn by intrigue and feud as his sons by different queens struggle for the succession. Bathsheba proves better than the rest of the schemers and Solomon becomes king. But the consequences are dire, for with his splendour and power come injustice and folly, and on his death the kingdom disintegrates. A lot comes from David seeing Bathsheba bathing on the roof.

A very different story about sin, with no hint of sex in it, is the story of Naboth's vineyard in 1 Kings 21. Naboth's vineyard is next door to King Ahab's palace in Samaria, and the king wants to extend the royal gardens. Naboth refuses to give up his' ancestral inheritance. Calling her husband a weak fool, Queen Jezebel arranges for Naboth to be accused of blasphemy and treason and has him stoned. Ahab, who knows nothing of his wife's plans until it is all over, takes possession of the vacant vineyard. Here the issues are injustice and oppression and the rights of the poor in relation to the state. Here, too, the consequences are more than they at first appear, for this is one more piece in the saga of conflict between the foreigner Jezebel and the old ways of Israel which is to climax in the fall of the dynasty, and eventually of the city of Samaria and of the kingdom itself.

In both stories we see the terrifying power of wickedness to destroy and to mar. Sin is more than David's personal moral failing, as it is more than Ahab's greed, and it is certainly wrong to equate sin and sex. Sin is woven into the fabric of society and life itself. In one sense David and Ahab are just two more victims: but the damage from their wrongdoing is lasting and widespread.

These two stories give us examples of sin and sins: but sin also threads through the whole story-line of the Old Testament. God creates the world, and it is good. He creates a man and a woman, loves them and entrusts them with power and responsibility. But soon they are estranged from each other, from God, and from the natural world. The original harmony is gone. After that things get worse and violence spirals. God regrets what he has done and decides to wipe everything out with a flood and start again with a new nucleus: but no sooner has the water subsided than things start to go wrong again. This time God takes a different line, and decides on a long-term strategy to put matters right through one man and his descendants (Genesis 1–11). But the sorry story of sin repeats itself in Abraham's descendants: arrogant Joseph and his brothers who try to get rid of him (Genesis 29–50), their numerous descendants freed from Egypt by God who complain against Moses and turn to other gods (Exodus and Numbers), the tribes settling in Canaan and deserting the God who has given them their new land (Joshua and Judges), and then all through the history of the united kingdom and then the divided states until first the one and then the other is exiled (1 and 2 Samuel, 1 and 2 Kings). Why? According to the storyteller, it is because they have sinned and 'done that which was evil in the sight of the Lord' (e.g. 2 Kings 23.37). From beginning to end, from creation to exile, it is a story of sin.

This is not, of course, the whole story, for running alongside it is also the 'old, old story' of God and his love, of his work to save and deliver his people, to rescue them and to give them peace; the story of salvation. But that sin is a real part of the story, and equally a real part of our story, cannot be denied. Whether sin is defined as 'missing the mark' and 'falling short' of what we ought to be, as deliberate rebellion against God, breaking his rules and going against him, or as being wrong or doing wrong hardly matters, for it can be any or all of these, and more. And it is not confined to human wrongdoing, it is woven into the whole fabric of the world's life. For in the Bible sin is a fact of life; it is there, and life is marred and spoiled by it. This is fact; this is the way the world is and the way we are.

So what does God do about sin? The Old Testament story tells us that God tries to prevent it, as we shall see in our discussion of Psalm 103.18, but failing that he attempts to destroy it or to disarm it. He does this in two ways, either by punishing sinners (v. 9) or by forgiving them (vv. 3, 8, 10-13). Either way he tries to eradicate the sin which has so badly infected his creation. There are difficulties in the idea of God forgiving sin and people differ considerably, as we shall see, in what they think this means and how they understand that it is done: but the psalmist believes fervently that God forgives sins, and that God has forgiven his sin. He knows that 'all of his iniquity' is forgiven. This is cause for joy and thanksgiving. It is the first of God's blessings which he enumerates; his first reason for blessing the LORD, and we see here the generous and forgiving nature of God.

We have already thought a little about God's anger and suggested that it is a sign of his love, though admittedly there are stories in both the Old Testament and the New in which it looks as if God enjoys punishing people. Psalm 103.8-9 suggests that he doesn't; verse 8 says that he is 'slow to anger', or patient with sinful people, and verse 9 that he does not nurse his anger, or let it go on and on. His anger is a sign that he takes sin and evil seriously, hating their devastating effects on human life and the life of the world, but both Old Testament and New agree that God warns those who do wrong, and that if they stop doing wrong he forgives them.

According to the Old Testament God forgives those who are sorry for their sin and turn away from it, and so he has provided forms of worship for people to confess their sin, express their repentance and then 'hear the word of grace and the assurance of pardon'. The complex sacrifices in Leviticus 4.1–6.7 show how this was to be done. Some time after the Exile the great Day of Atonement became the important focus for this confession and absolution, when the High Priest led the rituals to 'make atonement' for the Temple, the priests and all the people (Leviticus 16). For Jews today this is the most solemn day of the year, and follows 10 days of fasting and penitence. These services show that sin is to be taken seriously, but we should also recognize that, according to Leviticus, these forms of service have been given by God so that the damage done by sin can be put right. 1 Kings 8.30-53, which is part of King Solomon's prayer at the dedication of the Temple, is an excellent example of the people's belief in a forgiving God. Psalms 32, 85 and 130 may be some of the words for confession, absolution and thanksgiving. Clearest of all is the statement in 2 Chronicles 7.14, part of a later version of how Solomon came to build the Temple. In a vision he hears God say:

> If my people who are called by my name
> humble themselves, pray, seek my face,
> and turn from their wicked ways, then I
> will hear from heaven, and will forgive
> their sin and heal their land.

Notice the point in the last line which is so obvious to the writer that it does not need to be spelled out. Because people have 'sinned' and done 'wicked' things the land has become sick or diseased. If people repent forgiveness will follow, and the land too will be 'healed'. Included in this package are rules for making amends, for it is no good for a thief to say that he is sorry while he holds on to the proceeds of his theft (Leviticus 6.2-7). There has to be restitution or compensation and there has to be 'amendment of life'. If there is a genuine desire to repent, God strengthens those who repent, and his forgiveness of sinners includes the grace and strength to enable them to walk in newness of life. All of this shows that God is 'slow to anger', and that his anger need not be the last word.

Psalm 51 is a beautiful example of these ideas brought together in an individual psalm of confession. The editors of the book of Psalms call this a 'Psalm of David', and say that David sang these words 'when the prophet Nathan came to him, after he had gone in to Bathsheba'. They set the psalm on the lips of the rapist king who now realizes the wrong he has done. It begins with an appeal to God's forgiving goodness:

> Have mercy on me, O God, according to your
> steadfast love;
> according to your abundant mercy blot out
> my transgressions.
> Wash me thoroughly from my iniquity,
> and cleanse me from my sin. (vv. 1-2)

'David' knows that God is rightly angry at his appalling behaviour (vv. 4, 8, 11) but also that God is a God of 'mercy', 'steadfast love' and 'abundant mercy', the same three words we find in Psalm 103.8, and to him he confesses his 'transgressions', 'iniquity' and 'sin', the same three words we find in Psalm 103.10-11. David confesses his sin and asks not only for forgiveness, but also for complete renewal, a clean heart, and a new and right spirit (Psalm 51.10). This psalmist also knows that offering sacrifices by themselves are of no use, and that repentance is essential, that 'the sacrifice acceptable to God is a broken spirit; a broken and contrite heart, O God, you will not despise' (Psalm 51.17).

There are, however, limits to forgiveness and cases where God's anger is the last word. There can be no forgiveness without repentance, and those who sin 'high-handedly', who go on doing what they clearly know to be wrong, can expect no forgiveness at all (Numbers 15.30-31). Society needs to be protected from people like this. If people will not do as they ought to do, when they have been told quite plainly what that is, or if they will not stop doing wrong when they have been warned, then action needs to be taken for the good of everyone else. It was, therefore, the responsibility of the king to ensure that society was protected from such people, and the king was seen as the lynch-pin of the whole integrated system of law and order, morality, culture and religion (Psalm 72.1-4). But if the king was embroiled in the wrongdoing, then, according to the likes of the preachers Amos or Jeremiah, God had no alternative but to punish the whole people in an attempt to wipe out the cancer of evil. God would threaten and he would warn, and forgiveness would be granted if there was repentance, but if there was not these prophets insisted that the people had only themselves to blame, they had brought their destruction on themselves (Jeremiah 36.1-3). Sin and evil is simply too serious and deadly to ignore. But if there is repentance, which is what God wants, then this is met with forgiveness:

> He does not deal with us according to our sins, nor repay us according to our iniquities. (Psalm 103.10)

Sin and evil make God angry but that anger need not be the last word, for his anger does not last 'for ever' and he does not go on prosecuting his case against those who do evil if they recognize their guilt. Those who do not 'fear the LORD' will presumably get exactly what their sins deserve. God will deal with them 'according to their sins' and repay them 'according to their iniquities', he will not 'remove' their transgressions at all (v. 12). What this means and how God will punish such people the psalmist does not say. He is no preacher of hellfire and damnation, gloating over the fate of the damned, for his purpose is to sing of the good news of God's forgiveness and help. So the psalmist moves on to talk of God's dealings with those who repent. He sings confidently, and gives others words to sing, of the generosity of God which he has himself known. Here is a plain statement about the forgiveness of sins, that God does not deal with us according to our sins or repay us according to our iniquities. The meaning is simple, and verse 12 expresses it equally plainly: God puts our transgressions as far away from us 'as the east is from the west'. The psalmist does not explain how God forgives sins, just as he does not explain how God punishes sinners. He simply gives thanks that it is so. God does not punish those who turn to him as they deserve to be punished, he forgives them. This is a bold and sweeping statement of fact. But it is more than that. It is a succinct and simple statement of what the Old Testament teaches everywhere. Psalm 130.3 puts it like this:

> If you, O LORD, should mark iniquities,
>   Lord, who could stand?
> But there is forgiveness with you, so that
>   you may be revered.

In one sense we have said everything that needs to be said: but because of certain trends in Christianity today it is necessary to go into the question of forgiveness a little more deeply. We need to look at the question of how God forgives sin.

If we were to ask the psalmist to explain how God forgives sin, he would talk, as we have seen, about repentance and special services of worship, and, most importantly of these, the Day of Atonement. If we pressed him further he would describe the details of these services, which were sacrifices of varying kinds. Different animals would be killed depending on what had gone wrong, and depending on the wealth of the person involved. A very poor person would not even bring an animal; for them two kilos of flour was quite acceptable; wealthier people brought animals. The worshipper would put his hand on the animal's head before handing it over to a priest to slaughter. A drop of blood would be smeared on the altar and the rest poured out on the ground at the base of the altar, or splashed against the sides. The fat would be carefully collected and burned to smoke on the altar. The rest of the carcass would be burned outside the Temple. The rules talk about two different services, a 'sin-offering' and a 'guilt-offering', but the difference between them is not explained and the rituals are the same (Leviticus 7.7). As well as offering a sacrifice, the guilty person would need to make restitution. The Day of Atonement was a state occasion and so everything was on a bigger scale, and there were also one or two extras (Leviticus 16). There was special incense and the High Priest smeared the blood on the 'mercy seat' inside the Holy of Holies in the Temple, a sacred place entered only once a year in this service. The main difference was that two goats were chosen, one was offered as a sacrifice and the other was driven out into the wilderness 'carrying their iniquities to a barren region' and set free (Leviticus 16.22). The purpose of this day is summed up in Leviticus 16.30: '... on this day atonement shall be made for you, to cleanse you; from all your sins you shall be clean before the LORD'.

'Atonement' is the word we use for this 'covering up' of sin, its removal and disarming. It is God's will that the scourge or contamination of sin should be removed and that people should be set free from the burden of their own wrongdoing, and so he gives these services as the opportunity for people to confess their sin and to know that their sin has been taken away and their guilt removed. The Old Testament sees these services as gifts of God out of his love. God saved them from Egypt through Moses, and gives them these services as part of his *Torah*, (usually translated as his 'Law', but better as 'Teaching' or 'Guidance') so that they can now continue to enjoy their new freedom and peace. The rules and regulations set out what should be done, but they do not say how these actions bring about forgiveness. What they do say is that the person who does these things is forgiven (Leviticus 4.20, 26, 31, 35 etc.), and that through the Day of Atonement services the nation is 'cleansed' from all its sin. Basic to these services is the requirement that the worshippers are 'repentant', genuinely sorry for their wrongdoing and sincere in their intention to turn away from that sort of behaviour and not to do it again (Leviticus 26.40-41). Providing that they have also made restitution they hear 'the word of grace and the assurance of pardon'. Their sins are forgiven and they can go in peace, because that is what God wants for them.

The whole sacrificial system of the Old Testament is impossible for modern westerners to understand. It is part of an ancient and alien world which is entirely foreign to our ways of thinking. Even the Old Testament itself is not entirely clear on what was to be done, and certainly does not go into detailed explanations of why. There was obviously a belief that blood was somehow sacred, and was therefore on no account to be eaten, so special rules for killing animals for food were necessary, and in the middle of some of these rules we find one verse which says why blood is important in the sacrifices. Leviticus 17.11 reads:

> For the life of the flesh is in the blood;
> and I have given it to you for making
> atonement for your lives on the altar; for,
> as life, it is the blood that makes
> atonement.

Blood is the secret of life and the source of life, so when blood is offered on the altar the worshipper is giving God everything and the blood represents total dedication. But what it is especially important to notice in this verse is that God says that he has given the blood and the whole service in which it is offered on the altar as a means of putting everything right and dealing with sin and guilt. Sacrifices are not rituals thought up by us to attempt to win God's favour or change his mind, but liturgies that he has given to help us back to full life. Another mistake we make is to assume that sacrifice always involves blood and is always to do with sin. As we have seen, flour could be used in a sacrifice, and offerings of oil and incense were also accepted. And sacrifice was not always connected with sin; it was the normal form of Temple worship for every occasion. Harvest Thanksgiving was celebrated with sacrifices, as were personal thanksgivings and praise and also the daily Morning and Evening Prayers. Though we might find the thought repulsive and the sights, sounds and smells of the Temple repugnant, the underlying theology of the Temple worship is the same as our understanding of worship today. It is that God is to be worshipped, and that the worship of God is one of his gifts to us whereby we can have fellowship with him. Sacrifice accompanied worship. All that changed when the Romans destroyed the Temple in 70 AD, and in the Judaism of today worship through sacrifices in the Temple has been replaced by worship in the synagogues which is remarkably like much Christian worship in churches, with hymns, readings and prayers, and special events on special days. On the Day of Atonement today, confession is made in prayer and fasting, and repentance is the theme of the solemn synagogue services which last for most of the day.

If we pressed the psalmist for an answer in words of one syllable to the question of how God forgives and why, he would perhaps make a tart comment on the silliness of the question. God forgives because he loves. He forgives his Israelite children just like any normal parent would forgive their children. Love is like that. When his children come to him seriously sorry for their wrongdoing, ready to learn from their mistakes, promising not to do those things again, and having done what they can to put things right for those they have wronged, then he forgives them like any parent would. And that ought to be enough. Why does God forgive? Because he's like that!

But here we encounter another Christian misunderstanding. It is expressed in two verses of the hymn 'There is a green hill far away':

> He [Jesus] died that we might be forgiven,
> He died to make us good,
> That we might go at last to heaven,
> Saved by his precious blood.
>
> There was no other good enough
> To pay the price of sin;
> He only could unlock the gate
> Of heaven and let us in.

This hymn from the Victorian evangelical tradition has found its way into many hymn books and become very popular. It appears to represent both acceptable and orthodox Christian teaching and the faith of ordinary Christians. Its thinking is plain: Jesus had to die in order that God might forgive us. Without Jesus' death the gates of heaven would have remained shut. If the price of sin had not been paid there would have been no forgiveness. It was the death of Jesus that bought or won forgiveness and heaven for us. These are very crude ideas, and the picture of God they present is not a pleasant one. God is in heaven and the gates are shut on the inside. He is only persuaded to open them, with great reluctance, when Jesus pays the price by dying. If we add that Jesus was God's Son whom he sent 'to die for us', because God loves us so much, that only makes the picture worse: this god is not only unpleasant, but guilty of the murder of his own son as well. Do we really want to worship a god like that? We would have serious doubts about any human parent who behaved in this way, and whilst God is obviously more than a human parent, he is not less!

One particularly dangerous way that this argument is used is in much popular evangelism. The standard argument goes like this. It is in two parts:

1. We are sinners. Sin separates us from God because God is pure and holy. He hates sin. He cannot and will not look on sin. We can do nothing about this; we cannot remove the barrier or save ourselves. But God loves us and 'gave his only Son, that whoever believes in him should not perish but have eternal life' (John 3.16).

2. Jesus Christ's death is the way that the barrier of sin between us and God is removed and we are saved. This works because God's character is like a coin with two sides: his justice on the one side, and his love on the other. His justice condemns us, for sin must be punished. His love wants to forgive us. And on the cross his justice and his love were

perfectly satisfied. Sin had to be punished, so God in his love sent his Son to die in our place, bearing the death penalty our sins deserved. Jesus took the full punishment for our sin, and our debt was paid. So God can forgive us because Jesus has paid the price.

I have no problem with part 1 but, if we take any notice of the Old Testament at all, part 2 is fatally flawed. Its understanding of God is quite at odds with that of the Old Testament. God is no longer the holy and caring Father of Psalm 103 who does indeed hate sin but deals with it by calling his children to repent, and in whom there is no separation between justice and love. He has become the cold and hard 'judge' of the Roman world in which there is no such thing as forgiveness because crimes have to be paid for, or the feudal tyrant whose honour has to be 'satisfied'.

Fortunately the God and Father of our Lord Jesus Christ is the God of Abraham, Isaac and Jacob; and the God of the New Testament is the God of the Old Testament. This God did indeed send his Son because he loves us, so that those who believe might find eternal life. John 3.16 is too precious a verse to be allowed to be hijacked by this way of thinking, especially when it is quoted as in the argument above, as if it only talks about Jesus' death. It speaks about the whole life and mission of Jesus, who spent his ministry seeking and saving the lost (Luke 19.10) and calling people to repent and return to God (Mark 1.15). The end of this ministry, on earth at least, was that he died on the cross. In the New Testament there are various explanations of Jesus' death, but none of them say that it was in order that 'we might be forgiven' or to 'pay the price of sin' in the way that the hymn implies. He did not have to die before God would or could forgive us. The cross does speak of God's love, a love that will not let us go, and a love showed by Jesus himself right to the end as he prayed for the forgiveness of those who were nailing him to the cross (Luke 23.34).

The blood of the cross is as powerful a symbol in the New Testament as the blood of the sacrifices was in the Old Testament, but Christ's blood no more wins our forgiveness from God than the blood of the Temple sacrifices did. Christ's blood does not obtain our forgiveness, it declares it; just as the blood of the sacrificed animals was a sign of forgiveness. The death of Jesus did not change God's mind, any more than the deaths of those animals changed God's mind, for his mind did not need to be changed; he was on our side in any case. The death of Jesus was a declaration of our forgiveness, an assurance of pardon. In this way, and in this way only, can the death of Jesus on the cross be said to have anything to do with forgiveness at all.

The Bible does not give one single answer to the question of why Jesus died on the cross, and exploring that question would also take us too far away from the Old Testament, but Psalm 103 gives a very clear answer to why he didn't. He did not die so that God could forgive us, for God's hands are not tied by sin. Sin hurts God, it offends him and he hates it: but he can, and he does, forgive. In Psalm 103.10 the psalmist expresses his joyful amazement at this and rejoices in God's free forgiveness. In this black and white sentence he says boldly that God 'does not deal with us according to our sins, nor repay us according to our iniquities'. We do not get what we deserve from God! He is a God of forgiveness and of grace, and to drive his point home the psalmist follows his statement with two pictures which emphasize God's generosity: he 'removes our transgressions from us' and he 'has compassion on us'.

Finally, verse 14 gives another slant on the human condition:

> For he knows how we were made; he remembers that we are dust.

Psalm 103 is about the LORD's love. It begins with the psalmist giving testimony to God's love as he had experienced it. It continues in verse 8, quoting the old mini-creed about the love of God. In verses 9-13 it stresses how amazing this love of God is. So if we ask why God loves, the answer seems to be that he loves because he is God. Fathers love because they are fathers, it goes with the role. God loves because he is God, it goes with the role. But suddenly the psalm comes down to earth, saying that God loves us, 'because he knows how we were made; he remembers that we are dust'. The psalmist seems to say that God loves us particularly because of our vulnerability and our frailty.

Behind this verse lies that second creation story and Genesis 2.7 in particular. God 'forms' a male human being out of 'dust', and those two words are found in this verse in the psalm, 'because he knows how we were *formed*; he remembers that we are *dust*'. The human condition is one of 'dust' or 'the dust of the ground' (Genesis 2.7). That is not to say that the psalmist who wrote Psalm 103 is not also aware of the beauty, wonder and greatness of human life, for we have already seen in verse 4 that he says that God has treated us like kings and queens, an allusion to the creation psalm, Psalm 8. But this does not prevent him from writing that we are 'dust', that dust is what we are made of and dust is what we are. He does not mean that we are 'dirty' but that we are frail and insubstantial, as we see in Psalm 78.39 where the same point is made. We are 'frail children of dust, and feeble as frail'. There is nothing to us. The dust on the ground is so light that the wind blows it everywhere. Dust can lie on a pair of scales and make not the slightest difference to their accuracy (Isaiah 40.15). We are about as weighty as that! Our bodies are made of the commonest thing there is – dust – and when we die that is where they return, 'ashes to ashes, dust to dust' as the Burial Service says, quoting Genesis 3.19. And that is where everyone returns, for death is the great leveller (Psalm 22.29). We are only dust, a beautiful antidote to human pride and pretension. God knows all of this, the psalmist seems to imply, and so he sees our transgressions, iniquities and sins as signs of our weakness and frailty. He hardly expects anything else. There is something of the inevitable about our weakness and our failures. God knows how easy it is for us to sin and he accepts that. He has no illusions about our ability to be the sort of people he wants us to be. He recognizes that it is part of our human nature to fail and he accepts that; 'he knows our frame' as older translations put it, and acknowledges our human weakness.

There is something very liberating about this verse, especially against the background of a success-oriented society like ours, and in all probability like the psalmist's own. God understands failure. The verse also helps us to keep our sin in perspective, for Christianity since St Augustine in the fourth century has always been in danger of paying too much attention to it. In God's eyes it is not the most important part of what we are, nor is it the least important part. God deals with it by forgiving and putting it away from us, as the psalm has already noted (vv. 8-13) and by giving us a framework in which to live and work, as the psalmist will explain next (vv. 15-18).

Questions for reflection:

1. What do you think about the picture of God painted in 'There is a green hill far away'?

2. Have you ever thought about sacrifice in the way that it is discussed in this chapter? Does it make sense to think of sacrifice as God's gift to us, rather than as our attempt to influence him?

3. Forgiveness seems to be very important both in Psalm 103 and in Christianity. Why do you think this is? And what would you feel if we did not have a prayer of confession and a declaration of forgiveness in every service of worship?

4. The Old Testament expects people to take repentance seriously. Do we?

5

Responding to this God

Psalm 103 is an invitation to 'bless the LORD', to offer to God our praise and thanksgiving in worship and our lives in dedication. He is a generous God whose love is steadfast, who acts to put things right and restore what is wrong, and who offers forgiveness to all who admit their need of it. He takes the initiative to bless and save, and the psalmist calls on his hearers to respond by being grateful and living faithful lives.

The psalm speaks of those who live such lives in a number of ways. In verses 13 and 17 those who 'bless the LORD' and offer him their total commitment are referred to as 'those who fear the LORD', in the rather misleading and old-fashioned wording of the NRSV. The *Good News Bible* is much better, it calls them 'those who honour' the LORD. This common Old Testament expression certainly does not mean those who cower in terror before a frightening God.

There are ways in which God is frightening, and there are times when those who worship God come before him in awe and wonder and with 'fear and trembling'. Any religion which has no sense of the 'otherness' of God, no shrinking or stammering before the power or purity of God, is missing something. The 'fear of the LORD' probably meant that kind of thing at first, but in most places in the Old Testament 'those who fear the LORD' refers to those who 'honour' God or, simply, those who 'worship' him. 'The fear of the LORD is the beginning of wisdom' is a motto in parts of the Old Testament (e.g. Proverbs 9.10, 15.33, Psalm 111.10, Job 28.28) and there the phrase can be translated by 'religion' or 'acknowledging God' or just 'faith', because what the motto means is that anyone who wants to be wise should begin by taking God seriously! Those who do that do as he requires (Psalms 103.17-18, 112.1) and they also worship (Psalms 22.23, 66.16, 115.11, 135.20). Not everyone does or did, and though God's love is not confined to them, they are the ones who have recognized that they have received it and responded accordingly.

Psalm 103.18 describes such people as 'those who keep his covenant, and remember to do his commandments'. Let's take the second half of this verse first, but we need to be alert here. The psalmist is not saying that if we keep the covenant and the commandments then God will love us, though that is how 'Old Testament religion' is sometimes described. Keeping the covenant and doing the commandments is not a condition of receiving the love of God. For the psalmist the covenant and the commandments are God's generous gifts, given so that through them we can continue to experience God's blessings. We see this very clearly in the introduction to the Ten Commandments in Exodus 20.1-2 and Deuteronomy 5.6:

> And he said: I am the LORD your God,
> who brought you out of the land of Egypt,
> out of the house of slavery; you shall ...
> you shall not ...

The Ten Commandments and the covenant of which they are part come after God has brought the Israelites out of Egypt. He does not say, 'If you will ... and providing you do not ... then I will save you.' He has already delivered them from Egypt, and they have already experienced his love and care, his generous grace. These commandments come after salvation, not before. God loves us first and then, when we have learned that, he gives us guidelines so that we can continue to enjoy the good life which he has given us. So Moses is given the commandments to pass on to the people, so that they can continue to enjoy the fullness of life that is God's purpose for them. Exodus 20.2 puts the Ten Commandments and the other laws which follow them into proper perspective, and gives the lie to mistaken ideas about 'the Law' which are still found.

There are a number of words for this guidance and advice in the Old Testament including 'statutes', 'ordinances', and 'commandments', but the key one is *Torah*, usually translated as 'law'. For a Jew keeping *Torah*, which is used both for this teaching in general and as the name for the first five books of the Hebrew Bible which encapsulate it, is neither a burden to be doggedly borne nor a means of earning God's favour. Instead it is a grateful response to what God has done, it is 'gospel', the good news of how a saved people can joyfully sing to their Saviour. We sometimes find it hard to see things in this way for the word 'law' has had a bad press in Christianity. We have been conditioned to think of 'the law' as the opposite of 'the gospel'; that the Old Testament is about 'law' but the New is about 'grace'. We accuse the Pharisees of seeking 'salvation by works' instead of accepting the teaching of Jesus and St Paul that 'salvation is by grace'. Law is bad and negative, the opposite of faith which is good and positive. But to see what the Old Testament, the Pharisees and Judaism mean by *Torah* we can read Psalm 119, the longest psalm of all. From beginning to end it is about the psalmist's delight in God's *Torah* and his grateful thanks for God's gift of it. Time and time again the psalmist says that God's *Torah* is his delight, as in verse 97: 'O, how I love your law! It is my meditation all day long.' Likewise the Jewish celebration of *Simchat Torah:* 'Rejoicing for the *Torah*' is another good way of seeing what the 'Law' means to a Jew and in the Old Testament. This is the festival at the end of the year when the readings from the *Torah* scroll come to an end and, before they start again, the scroll is carried with singing and dancing around the synagogue, and even out into the streets. And you don't go dancing around with a book of rules! It is best not to translate *Torah* as 'law' at all; words like 'revelation', 'teaching', 'guidance' are better. 'Gospel' is perhaps the best one of all.

So in verse 18 the psalmist follows the good news, gospel, of the LORD's steadfast love by saying that it is to those who 'remember to do his commandments'. In the story of the making of the covenant on Mount Sinai the giving of the Ten Commandments has a prominent place, but the number of the commandments does not end at 10. In the chapters that follow many others are found, and the Rabbis counted 613 altogether in the '*Torah* of Moses'. To us they seem an odd mixture. Some are to do with methods of worship: which festivals are to be observed, the offering of sacrifices, or who are to be priests and what they have to do. Others concern crimes: criminal acts like theft or murder, and also things like slander or negligence. Other rules regulate social practices like divorce, banking or slavery. Then there are rules covering diet and cooking, what sort of animals can be eaten, and how they are to be prepared. The purpose of some of these laws is obvious; any civilized society needs laws about murder, and any religion needs rules about worship: but the Old Testament makes no distinctions between what we would call criminal law, ritual rules, civil law or morals. God has given all the commandments as guidelines for how society can organize itself for the peace and well-being (*shalom*) of all, and how individuals can live happily together. God's covenant people receive these guidelines as a gift. It is important to note here that the Old Testament does not distinguish between religion and the rest of life. These commandments cover all of life. Belief and behaviour go together, and grateful faithfulness to God is lived out just as much in the kitchen as in the temple. A verse of my favourite hymn sums up the kind of living which this gift make possible:

> So shall no part of day or night
> From sacredness be free;
> But all my life, in every step,
> Be fellowship with thee.

The first part of Psalm 103.18 speaks of this as 'keeping the covenant', and 'covenant' ought to begin with a capital letter. The Covenant which the psalmist has in mind is the one made between God and the people of Israel, with Moses as the go-between, on Mount Sinai after Moses had brought the people out of Egypt. As God had acted in a special way to save his people, in the Covenant God had committed himself to them, and they had committed themselves to him in a new and unique way. They had become God's Covenant People.

'Covenants' in Israel and its surrounding cultures were agreements, or contracts, ranging from marriage contracts, to trade agreements, to international treaties. Two parties entered into an agreement, or 'made a covenant'. Such agreements might be between two equal parties, like the kings Solomon of Israel and Hiram of Tyre (1 Kings 5.12), or they might be between two very unequal ones, such as between God and the people. Sometimes there might be few, if any, terms and conditions, and the covenant might look like an unconditional promise; at other times there might be a long list. So in the Old Testament we find God pictured as getting involved with people. He makes a covenant with Noah and all the living things on earth after the

Flood, that never again will he destroy the world in that way (Genesis 9.8-17). This is a solemn and simple promise or pledge, and Noah has to do nothing but listen to it and be grateful. God also makes two covenants with Abraham. In the first he promises Abraham that the land through which he is travelling will one day belong to his descendants (Genesis 15.17-19). In the second he repeats that promise and emphasizes that the old man and his barren wife will have a child, and that through this child his descendants will become a great nation (Genesis 17.1-14). This time he asks Abraham to show his commitment by undergoing circumcision, which from then on will be the distinguishing mark of all Abraham's descendants. God made a covenant, too, with the royal house of David, that a king of David's line would reign for ever in Jerusalem (Psalm 89.28-37). And during the Exile the prophet Jeremiah looks forward to a new covenant between God and his people, because the people had broken the old Mosaic one (Jeremiah 31.31-34).

The story of that Covenant begins in Exodus 19 and fills the rest of Exodus as far as chapter 33. It is a long and fascinating story. Moses shuttles back and forward, up and down the mountain, negotiating and renegotiating between God and the people. The scene shifts constantly between mountain top and plain, between Moses terrified by God's power and the Israelites bored with waiting around. Lists of rules interrupt moments of high drama. The heart of the matter is captured in the introduction in Exodus 19.3-6:

> Then Moses went up to God; the LORD called to him from the mountain, saying, 'Thus you shall say to the house of Jacob, and tell the Israelites: You have seen what I did to the Egyptians, and how I

bore you on eagles' wings [does Psalm
103.5 have an echo of this?] and brought
you to myself. Now therefore, if you obey
my voice and keep my covenant, you
shall be my treasured possession out of
all the peoples. Indeed, the whole earth is
mine, but you shall be for me a priestly
kingdom and a holy nation. These are the
words that you shall speak to the
Israelites.'

The LORD has rescued the Israelites from Egypt,
and on Mount Sinai he promises them that they will
be his special people if they are obedient to him and
do what he requires, if they 'obey his voice and keep
his covenant'. The terms of the covenant are the Ten
Commandments and the other rules and regulations
which go with them, and the people commit
themselves to keeping these laws (Exodus 24.7). In a
ceremony at the foot of the mountain there is
sacrifice and the splashing of the altar and the people
with the blood of the sacrificed animals, the 'blood of
the covenant' (Exodus 24.8). So the LORD and the
people of Israel are united; he is their God, they are
his people. He has saved them from Egypt, and has
offered them an ongoing blessing as his special
people; they have accepted this offer and they are
now God-and-people, so from now on they have a
contract with privileges and responsibilities on both
sides. In Psalm 103 the psalmist sings of this
covenant with joy. He belongs to this covenant-
people and invites all those who share that blessing to
join in witnessing to the way that those who have
kept to the contract have enjoyed what was promised,
that they have continued to experience the LORD's
steadfast love.

In covenant living belief and behaviour go
together, but Psalm 103 does not end on that note,

important though it is. It ends on the note of worship. The psalmist calls on all the company of heaven and all creation to acknowledge the LORD as God over all, the king of the universe, and to worship him (vv. 19-22). In singing the psalm the worshippers have recognized the frailty and failings of their human condition, but they have also celebrated its greatness and goodness, which comes from the generosity of God's steadfast love. A worshipping congregation has sung its faith, remembered its past and renewed its hope in God. That is how worship should be; as God is honoured, faith is renewed and life affirmed. The end of the psalm reminds the singers that the God who is interested in the details of their lives, the one who is the LORD their God, is the God of the whole universe, who has the whole world and all eternity in his hands. He is transcendent. He is magnificent beyond what human minds can grasp or words express: but he can be worshipped and adored.

The picture of God exalted as king in heaven in verse 19 is an important one in the Old Testament, and Jesus takes it up in his teaching about the 'kingdom of God'. 'The LORD is king' is the opening phrase of Psalms 93, 97 and 99, and the same idea is found in Psalms 95, 96 and 98 which is why this cluster of psalms are sometimes called the 'Enthronement Psalms' as they seem to picture God enthroned as king. The LORD is the king who defeats the forces of chaos and death, pictured as mighty floods and surging 'waters' (Psalm 93.3-4). The LORD has imposed his rule on this chaos so the earth has been made firm and secure so that 'it shall never be moved' (Psalm 96.10). He is king of the whole earth, even to the farthest coastlands (Psalm 97.1) and the God of all nations (Psalm 96.10). He is king over all the gods (Psalms 95.3, 97.9). 'All the earth' is called to worship him (Psalms 96.1, 97.1, 98.4). His throne is set in heaven, surrounded by clouds, thick darkness, fire and lightning (Psalm 97.2-5). His royal will is to be obeyed (Psalm 93.5), and past disobedience is quoted as a warning (Psalm 95.8-9). Like a true king he has been the saviour and helper of his people in the past (Psalms 98.1-3, 99.4-9) and the psalmists rejoice because he is coming again 'to judge' (to save!) the earth and its people (Psalms 96.10-13, 97.10-12, 98.7-9).

Behind these pictures of God as the king of creation lies another old creation story, glimpsed elsewhere in the Old Testament, which Israel adapted from a widespread ancient Near Eastern picture of creation as the outcome of a battle between the gods and the monsters of chaos. Before the earth was formed there was God and his great enemy, a monster with various names, such as Rahab or Leviathan, the great monster of chaos and evil. They had fought. God had won. Out of the dead body of his defeated enemy God had made the heavens and the earth: life out of death, order out of chaos, good out of evil. Traces of this story remain in the Old Testament at Psalm 89.5-18, Isaiah 51.9-11 and in Job (7.12, 26.12 and 38.8-11), but it is best seen in Psalm 74.12-17. In the middle of a psalm which is lamenting the destruction of the Temple and what seems to be the LORD's helplessness or reluctance to do anything about it, the psalmist remembers God's power. God is the king who has defeated his enemies before and he can be expected to do it again.

Psalm 95.3 speaks of the LORD as a 'great God, and a great King above all gods' and this idea is found again in Psalm 82, which pictures the God of Israel as the President of the heavenly council, taking the chair in the assembly of the gods, and calling the rest of the gods to account for the way they have handled their responsibilities, especially towards the vulnerable and the needy. The Old Testament does not speak with one voice on the question of the existence of other gods beside the God of Israel. This psalm sees the God of Israel as the chief of the gods, and not as the only one there is, and this is in line with Deuteronomy 32.43 and 32.8-9. Other nations have other gods, but the God of Israel is supreme over these gods and their nations (Psalm 47.2-3). Other parts of the Old Testament disagree strongly and dismiss these other gods as idols. They are no gods at all, for the LORD is the only God there is. Isaiah of Babylon states this powerfully (Isaiah 44.6-8, 45.5-6, 18-22, 46.8-11), and words very like his are found in Deuteronomy 32.39: 'See now that I, even I, am he: there is no god besides me.' We can even see some ancient censorship on this topic. The official version of the Hebrew Bible in Deuteronomy 32.8 and 32.43 now contains no reference to other gods at all. It talks about 'the number of the sons of Israel', but the first Greek translation of the Old Testament had 'the number of the angels of God' and a Hebrew manuscript from the Dead Sea Scrolls has 'the number of the sons of God', so NRSV goes for 'the number of the gods'. Interesting. The orthodox belief of Judaism which Christianity and Islam inherited is that the LORD is the one and only God, but this would not have been agreed by every writer whose words or ideas have been preserved in the Old Testament.

The psalmist insists that it is the LORD who is king, and that the LORD is king over all, that there are no final limits to his dominion or his authority. Those who sang the psalm might think of the king of creation's victory over chaos and death, and link this with their personal recovery from illness or their experience of forgiveness. Or they might meditate on how the King of Israel delivered their ancestors through the Exodus, and gave them his *Torah*, and so remember with joy that they are now his people, or with confession that they have forsaken his covenant and neglected his commandments. Those who were oppressed, or afraid or despondent might find hope and comfort in the psalmist's assurance that the LORD is indeed king. The ending of the psalm begins with a pointed reminder of the seriousness and joy of worship, of the obligations and the privileges of religion and of its hope and challenge.

In the Temple, singing this psalm, the worshippers glimpse the situation as it really is, that the LORD's throne is 'established', set firm and immovable, and by their worship they are strengthened to live as the people of God, the loyal and loved subjects of the king of heaven. Even though it is obvious that God's kingdom has not come and his will is not done here on earth, and that there are many things here that do not conform to his will and purpose, yet the psalm sounds a note of hope, that one day God will reign as king over all. As he does now in the heavens, and in the Temple, so he will on earth. The obedience of the worshippers in the Temple and their peace and blessing is a foretaste of what it will be like for all on earth when God is finally acknowledged as king. In the end, he asserts, goodness will triumph over evil, light over darkness and life over death. Generations of Jews have not lived to see this and yet the belief that this will one day be so has sustained them in their faith through the most terrible of persecutions over many centuries. Likewise generations of Christians have not lived to see the final triumph of good over evil, which we believe is promised in the cross of Jesus. This picture is a powerful encouragement to faith at times when faith is difficult. It urges us to endure to the end in the conviction that goodness will triumph. It expresses the certainty of God's ultimate victory.

And so the psalm calls on all the company of heaven and all of earth to 'bless the LORD':

Bless the LORD, O you his angels,
  you mighty ones who do his bidding,
    obedient to his spoken word. (v. 20)
Bless the LORD, all his hosts,
  his ministers that do his will. (v. 21)
Bless the LORD, all his works,
  in all places of his dominion. (v. 22)

The heavenly king sits on a throne and he is surrounded, as earthly kings are, by courtiers and royal officials: the 'angels' (v. 20) and the 'hosts' (v. 21) who are waiting to do whatever the king requires.

The Old Testament and its world have no problem in believing in God, gods and spirits, and in heaven, heavens and underworlds. There was the world in which people lived, the world of their senses, and even this world was full of wonders and strange things that defied the imagination and evoked awe and wonder. But there was also the unseen world, which was in many ways more real and certainly far more powerful than the world that could be seen. This was the world of God and the gods, of spirits and demons, of strange powers and forces. All ancient religion took this unseen world seriously. It was the world of magic, the paranormal and the occult: the world of the beyond which was also present everywhere in this world. The Old Testament shares this way of looking at things, and so has no problem with envisaging God, gods, a heavenly court, angels, cherubim and seraphim, spirits or ghosts, though it is remarkably restrained about some of these. It knows about the unseen world, but it doesn't pry too much into some parts of it. It knows that some people are admitted into the unseen world by dreams and visions, but that sort of thing is not to be encouraged, and dabbling with the occult is expressly forbidden to those who worship the LORD. But a preoccupation with the occult is one thing, a healthy imagination about 'all the company of heaven' is something else and, as in this psalm, an encouragement to faithful living in the here and now.

In places the Old Testament pictures God in heaven hidden by fire and smoke, in indescribable power and splendour, but occasionally this is seen on earth, as on Mount Sinai or in the Temple, or by those to whom a vision is granted. That world of heaven is in some ways the 'real' world, compared to which our world is one of passing shadows. A story of the prophet Elisha captures this perspective beautifully. The king of Aram (Syria) had sent his army to Dothan to capture the prophet because he kept seeing visions of their plans and telling the Israelite king what his enemies were planning:

> When an attendant of the man of God rose early in the morning and went out, an army with horses and chariots was all around the city. His servant said, 'Alas, master! What shall we do?' [Elisha] replied, 'Do not be afraid, for there are more with us than there are with them.' Then he prayed, 'O LORD, please open his eyes that he may see.' So the LORD opened the eyes of the servant, and he saw; the mountain was full of horses and chariots of fire all around Elisha. (2 Kings 6.15-17)

In the story the servant sees things only as they appear to be, but Elisha sees them as they really are because he could see the unseen world. It is this unseen world of ultimate reality that the psalmist is talking about in these verses in Psalm 103. In worship the congregation enters into this reality as it gathers in front of the very throne of heaven and is caught up with all the company of heaven in worship. Those who are singing the psalm in the Temple in Jerusalem audaciously call all that company of heaven to do as they are doing, to 'bless the LORD', to acknowledge that the LORD is God, and to worship him.

The 'angels' are called 'mighty ones' who do God's will (v. 20). The word translated 'angel' here means 'messenger' and is always translated as 'messenger' when these agents are sent by human beings. When it is God who is sending a message the messengers are called 'angels'. So angels crop up from time to time in Old Testament stories as God's messengers, often in pairs. Only very occasionally, and only in the book of Psalms, do they appear as anything other than messengers. Here we find 'guardian angels' who protect God's faithful people (Psalms 34.7, 91.11, compare 35.5), and the 'destroying angels' who punished the Egyptians before they would let the Israelites go (Psalm 78.49). Later on in Jewish literature angels become more common and more complicated, as such other Old Testament creatures as the cherubim and seraphim, or the 'sons of God', are drawn into the picture and also called 'angels'. There we find 'fallen angels' who wreak havoc on the earth after being expelled from heaven; and among the good angels there are different grades with different job descriptions, and more and more of them are named, such as Gabriel in the New Testament. The picture of angels as white singers with wings comes from Christian art of later centuries. In Psalm 103.20 these heavenly messengers are 'mighty ones', using a word for heroes or great soldiers. Even God's runabout messengers are terrifyingly great warriors.

The psalm then calls on all God's 'hosts' to join in and 'bless the LORD'. These are the ones who 'do his will', his 'ministers' or 'servants', a word used for servants like Elisha's servant at Dothan, for royal officials and for priests. But here we are still in heaven, and these are the 'heavenly host'. One of the titles for God in the Old Testament is 'the LORD of Hosts', which Christians are familiar with from the phrase 'Lord God of Sabaoth' in the old version of the Te Deum. Opinions differ as to what these hosts originally were. One view is that they are the 'celestial hosts' of sun, moon and stars. So to refer to the LORD as 'the LORD of Hosts' would be a way of saying that he was the God of the heavens, who created the hosts of the stars and controlled their movements (e.g. Psalms 8.3, 147.4), an ancient put-down directed at those who worshipped the sun, moon and stars as gods. This title would be a statement that these beautiful and mysterious heavenly bodies were not gods, just creatures that the great God, the LORD, had made. Another view is that the hosts in the title are the armies of Israel, his fighting host, and that the title refers to the LORD as the God of the hosts of Israel, 'Lord of armies, God of battles', or, as young David is said to have answered back to Goliath:

> You come to me with sword and spear and javelin; but I come to you in the name of the LORD of hosts, the God of the armies of Israel, whom you have defied.
> (1 Samuel 17.45)

The other suggestion notes that this title seems to have belonged especially to the Temple and is used in the Old Testament particularly where God is pictured as a king, which is exactly as we find it in Psalm 103. This view sees the 'hosts' of God as those numberless heavenly beings, including the angels, which surround God's throne, as in the vision of the prophet Micaiah ben Imlah in 1 Kings 22.19: 'I saw the LORD sitting on his throne, with all the host of heaven standing beside him to the right and to the left of him.'

From heaven in verse 21 the psalm comes down to earth in verse 22, from the unseen world to the world we see, but not simply to the human world. It calls on everything that the LORD has made, which is everything that there is, in every place where he 'rules', which is everywhere, to 'bless the LORD'. This appeal is worldwide, and to all creation. Each part of creation in its own way is to acknowledge the LORD, an idea found in other hymns of the Temple, such as Psalm 148.

The Old Testament talks about God as creator in a number of different ways, from the picture of the battle with the dragon to the solemn and orderly beauty of Genesis 1. At least four different creation stories can be found, and they are brought together in Psalm 104, a psalm in praise of God the creator and provider. In Psalm 103 the psalmist knows that his life is in the LORD's hands (vv. 2-5), not least because the LORD has formed him (v. 14) and given him life like a father (v. 13). He knows, too, that the LORD has been at work to save and help his people (vv. 6-7). The LORD is the active, creating and saving God of all creation, though as yet not everyone recognizes him or acknowledges him. In the closing verse of the psalm there is a note of hope that the day will come when God's kingdom will come 'on earth as it is in heaven', for 'the earth is the LORD's and all that is in it, the world, and those who live in it' (Psalm 24.1).

Questions for reflection

1. What impression does the phrase 'the fear of the LORD' make on you? Do you think we underplay the importance of the 'otherness' of God in our worship and faith today?

2. 'The commandments are God's good advice for the saved, not the conditions to be met before God will save.' Have you thought about it like that before?

3. We hear a lot these days about people's 'rights' and perhaps less than we should about their 'responsibilities'. Do you think that the Mosaic covenant balances the two?

4. These verses picture the worship of heaven, a common theme in our hymns. In what ways do you think this is a helpful picture? What are its shortcomings?

5. What do you think are the strengths and weaknesses of picturing God as a king?

6

Let us bless the LORD

Psalm 103 begins with the words:

> Bless the LORD, O my soul,
>   and all that is within me,
> bless his holy name.

And after calling on God's 'angels', his 'hosts' and 'all his works' to do the same it ends with the same words, 'Bless the LORD, O my soul.'

Bless the LORD

If we compare a variety of translations of this verse we find that the translation varies between 'bless', 'praise' and 'thank'. NRSV uses the more difficult and the most accurate of the three – 'bless' – but what does it mean to '*bless* the LORD'?

There is no problem with the idea of God blessing people. The Bible has plenty of examples, and most acts of worship include a 'Blessing' in one form or other. When ministers ask God's blessing on their congregations and on themselves at the end of a service, we have some idea about what this means. To pray for God to bless the congregation is to ask him to give his people whatever it is that they might need in order to live as his faithful people, so that everyone can leave the service filled with God's strength, joy and peace to live their lives for him in the following days. In the same way, when children are blessed at their baptism or dedication we know what is being done, that in a special way we are praying that their lives may be full and complete. We might wonder about how such blessings actually work, or even doubt if they work at all, but the idea is straightforward enough.

It gets more difficult to understand when we talk about 'blessing' things, like new church kitchens, memorial vases or wedding rings. But there is still something here about God doing something to the object. It might be that God gives a new quality, status or characteristic to the thing which has been blessed, but at the very least there is the suggestion that the thing blessed is somehow now dedicated to God or set apart with a special purpose in mind. It is more difficult to see what difference a blessing makes to an object, but most people who go in for blessing things do so presumably on the understanding that it does makes a difference of some sort.

But when it comes to 'blessing the LORD' it is not easy to see what it is that we are being asked to do. When God blesses a person, we believe that he gives that person something good which they did not have before, and on the face of it we do not have anything to give to God that he lacks. So many translations take the easy way out by translating the opening of Psalm 103 as 'Praise the LORD' or 'Thank the LORD', for the meaning of those phrases is clear enough. Easier and clearer, but wrong. The three verbs 'bless', 'praise' and 'thank' are closely related in English and in Hebrew, but they are not identical in meaning; they are not freely interchangeable and do not mean precisely the same thing, even if their meanings do overlap. To 'bless the LORD' is without doubt to do with thanking him, and with expressing that thanksgiving in public praise: but it is more than thanking him or praising him.

Psalm 34.1-3 shows what this extra something might be:

> I will bless the LORD at all times;
> his praise shall continually be in my mouth.

My soul makes its boast in the LORD;
   let the humble hear and be glad.
O magnify the LORD with me,
   and let us exalt his name together.

After saying that he will bless and praise the LORD, the psalmist talks about 'boasting' about God, 'magnifying the LORD' and 'exalting his name'. And when we note that the psalmists almost always talk about 'blessing the LORD' and very rarely about 'blessing God', we can see that the psalmist is making a point here, that the psalm is stressing the greatness of the LORD rather than of someone or something else. It is carefully emphasizing that it is the LORD who is to be blessed. Psalm 100.3 makes precisely the same point:

Know that the LORD is God.
It is he that made us, and we are his;
   we are his people, and the sheep of his
      pasture.

The same point is made in Psalm 135 which ends with a call to 'bless the LORD' because he is the only God, the rest are worthless idols (vv. 15-18); and in Psalm 145 which begins with the affirmation that the LORD is God and king, and as such he is to be blessed and praised. His great deeds, his majesty and his abundant goodness (vv. 7-9, and note that v. 8 is almost identical to Psalm 103.8) are the reasons for all creation to give thanks to God, and his faithful ones to bless him (v. 10). The psalm ends with the psalmist himself promising to praise God in the confident assurance that 'all flesh will bless his holy name for ever and ever' (v. 21).

1 Chronicles 29.10-11 and 20-22 also support this understanding of 'bless the LORD' where we see David '[blessing] the LORD' at a fund-raising event for

building the Temple. He makes an ascription of glory, to declare how great is the LORD. Declaring God's greatness (as in v. 11) is to bless the LORD. Similarly in verses 20-22 David calls on the congregation to 'bless the LORD'. Their response is to bow their heads, worship and offer sacrifices to God.

'Blessing the LORD' is about acknowledging him and giving him due honour. It is more than praising or thanking him, it is acknowledging the deity of the LORD, and affirming that he is God. This sense is clear in the use of the verb in other passages such as Exodus 18.10-12, Deuteronomy 8.10-20 and Joshua 22.33.

So what lies behind this emphasis? We know that it was a constant temptation for the people of Israel to worship other gods as well as 'the LORD your God who brought you out of the land of Egypt' (Exodus 20.2). That was the problem between the prophet Elijah and Queen Jezebel. As the King of Tyre's daughter, she brought her own god from Tyre as well as everything else a newly-married princess might bring when she moved into the palace in Samaria. She saw no problem in having any number of gods, and neither did her husband or most of the population of Israel. Elijah was the one who stood up to be counted for Israel's own God, but at one time he was so near to despair that he contemplated suicide, for he felt that he alone was the only real worshipper of Israel's true God. It is a make-or-break conflict, for at stake is not only a question of theology, but a whole system of morals and a lifestyle – for religion, life and politics are one. If Ahab follows Baal he is then free, for example, to take Naboth's vineyard by force (1 Kings 21) which threatens not only the LORD's will but the whole social fabric of Israel. And this is where the rigorous portrayal of the LORD as a 'jealous' God comes in (Exodus 20.5). He will share his divine status with no other and he demands the sole allegiance of his people, because otherwise the *shalom* of society is at risk. A century later the prophet Hosea fought the same battle, stressing that it is the LORD, Israel's own God, who has given the people all the blessings of a good harvest, and not the nature-god Baal, as so many of the people were apt to think (Hosea 2.8). This was a perennial problem, and here we see why 'blessing the LORD' means more than simply thanking or praising him. To 'bless the LORD' is to declare that he alone is God, the LORD and none other, as the people shouted in affirmation after Elijah's dramatic victory, 'The LORD indeed is God; the LORD indeed is God', or as the RSV puts it, 'The LORD, he is God; the LORD, he is God' (1 Kings 18.39).

We might, therefore, have something to give to God after all, for there is something which he lacks: our commitment. And that is our choice to give or withhold, as stories throughout the Bible show. God invites, humans respond or don't respond. Adoration, worship, love, commitment, discipleship, allegiance, faithful living in righteousness and justice are our gifts to God, for he cannot compel this way of living or extract it from us. It may well be that this is what it means to '*bless* the LORD', to give him our faith and life commitment by acknowledging that he is God.

Bless *the LORD*

In this book I have followed the convention used in the NRSV of putting 'LORD' in capital letters. Those capitals (and occasionally they appear as 'GOD') represent the personal name of God, which in the Hebrew appears as the four letters YHWH. Some older translations call him 'Jehovah' and two modern ones call him 'Yahweh', which is probably closer to how the name was pronounced. The problem is, however, that the name was never pronounced at all, it was far too holy to be spoken aloud. So in the synagogue readings this name was not spoken and '*Adonai*', 'The Lord', was said instead. Most English translations respect this ancient Jewish tradition by refusing to print the divine name and putting 'the LORD' instead.

So how did this personal name come to be known and what does it mean? One answer is given in the stories about Moses in Exodus 3 and 6. In Exodus 3 Moses is looking after his father-in-law's sheep, and in their wanderings they arrive at Mount Horeb, God's holy mountain (also called Mount Sinai). Here Moses sees a bush which is burning but not burning away, and when he goes to investigate he finds himself meeting the invisible God who commissions him to return to Egypt to rescue the Israelites from their slavery. He doesn't want to go, and one of his excuses is that he is not sure which God he is talking to, and so doesn't know what to say to the people when they ask him who has sent him. When God first confronted Moses he identified himself as 'the God of your father, the God of Abraham, the God of Isaac, and the God of Jacob' (Exodus 3.6). After listening to Moses' feeble excuses, he responds by saying, 'I AM WHO I AM' ... Thus you shall say to the Israelites, "I AM has sent me to you" ' (v. 14). Then for clarification he adds:

> 'Thus you shall say to the Israelites, "The LORD, the God of your ancestors, the God of Abraham, the God of Isaac, and the God of Jacob, has sent me to you ..." '
> (v. 15)

But despite all this Moses remains unconvinced and further excuses follow.

Much the same sort of thing is said in Exodus 6, which tells the story of Moses going back to God, complaining that nothing has worked out as God had planned. This time he is told to go back to the Israelites and tell them that God means what he says, and that he will rescue them from their slavery. In this dialogue (Exodus 6.2-3) God says:

> 'I am the LORD. I appeared to Abraham, Isaac, and Jacob as God Almighty [*El Shaddai*], but by my name "The LORD" I did not make myself known to them.'

This suggests that the name 'the LORD' is a new one, but we find God called by that name much earlier in the Old Testament story, by Eve, Lamech, Noah and Abraham himself (Genesis 14.22, 15.2). Here is an obvious inconsistency of some sort, and it illustrates how the story in Exodus was put together from various older stories, one of which called God 'the LORD' all the way through, and one which thought that that special name was first given to Moses. The final editor or editors blended the stories together without trying to tidy up these loose ends.

The message Moses is to give follows in Exodus 6.6-9, and it begins and ends in the same way:

> 'Say therefore to the Israelites, "I am the LORD, and I will free you from the burdens of the Egyptians ... I will bring you into the land that I swore to give to Abraham, Isaac and Jacob; I will give it to you for a possession. I am the LORD." '

The Israelites are to listen to Moses and to believe and do what he says because Moses speaks on behalf of 'the LORD'. So this name for their God is for ever to be associated with the great rescue that is about to take place, which will demonstrate that the LORD is indeed God, the powerful Lord of history and of the people of Israel.

What does this personal name mean? No real help is given in Exodus 3.14 with 'I AM WHO I AM', or simply, 'I AM' and the footnotes in the NRSV shows the further complication that this could also mean, 'I AM WHAT I AM' or 'I WILL BE WHAT I WILL BE.' In Hebrew this phrase is similar in some ways to the name 'Yahweh' – which is why NRSV puts them in capital letters too – but that is about all that can be said. Both the personal name and these two 'I AM' sayings are tied in somehow to the verb 'to be' but 'Yahweh' does not mean, 'I am who I am' nor 'I am', though it just might mean, 'He will be'. There seems to be a deliberate air of mystery about this name and its meaning.

Deuteronomy 6.4-5 are important verses in the Jewish Faith, for verse 4 is the key verse of the '*Shema*', the prayer which is recited going in or out of one's house, and in almost every service in the synagogue:

> Hear, O Israel: The LORD is our God, the
> LORD alone. You shall love the LORD your
> God with all your heart, and with all your
> soul, and with all your might.

We see the mystery of God's name in the core of this prayer which consists of only four Hebrew words, for another look at the NRSV footnotes shows that there are at least three other ways of translating the phrase: 'The LORD our God is one LORD', 'The LORD our God, the LORD is one' and 'The LORD is our God, the LORD is one.' The *Shema* clearly means that the LORD is to be the only God that Israel is to worship, but what else it means is not clear. Does it mean that the LORD is the only God there is? Or that he is unique among the other gods in some way? Or that he is somehow complete in himself, whole and entirely self-sufficient? There is no agreed answer to these questions, and that itself is important, for it reminds us that God is a mystery, and that all our talk about him and attempts to define him are bound to fail. He is beyond our powers to describe, or understand or even imagine. As St Paul reminds us:

> For now we see in a mirror, dimly, but then we will see face to face. Now I know only in part; then I will know fully, even as I have been fully known. (1 Corinthians 13.12)

Psalm 103 reflects this. It is a psalm of praise which affirms that the LORD is the one to be blessed, praised and thanked when the people of Israel gather for worship (vv. 1-2, 20-22). It remembers God's revelation to Moses (v. 7), and what he has done for his people (vv. 2-6, 10-13), acknowledging him for it. It also knows that God is mystery, enthroned in the heavens (vv. 19-21), 'high and lofty' as Isaiah of Jerusalem might say (Isaiah 6.1), and that he is as far beyond us as his eternity is from our mortality (vv. 11-17); 'For my thoughts are not your thoughts, nor are your ways my ways' as Isaiah of Babylon might put it (Isaiah 55.8-9).

The mystery of God is also reflected in the ending of the first verse of Psalm 103 which is a call to 'bless his holy name'. 'Name' here is only another way of saying that we should bless the LORD, and it is what is said about the LORD that is important here: that he is holy, i.e. mysterious, powerful and even frightening. 'Holy' is a frequently used word in the Old Testament, and means 'special', the opposite of ordinary. God is, of course, supremely special and out of the ordinary, so places or things to do with him are also special. The famous hymn 'Holy, holy, holy, Lord God Almighty!' puts it nicely when it says to God:

> Only thou art holy; there is none beside thee,
> Perfect in power, in love, and purity.

That hymn is based on Revelation 4.8-11, part of John's vision of the heavenly chorus singing their praise to God, but John got the idea from Isaiah of Jerusalem's great vision of God as king enthroned above the Temple in Isaiah 6, where the seraphim are calling to one another as they fly around God's mighty throne:

> 'Holy, holy, holy is the LORD of hosts;
>   the whole earth is full of his glory.' (Isaiah 6.3)

To say that God is holy is to think of his absolute perfection. 'Perfect in power' might have made the psalmist think of God as the creator of the world and as daily life-giver. 'Perfect in love' would have made him think of God's generous care for his people in delivering them from slavery in Egypt. 'Perfect in purity' would have made him conscious of his own sinfulness, just as Isaiah responded to his vision of the holy God by saying:

> 'Woe is me! I am lost, for I am a man of unclean lips, and I live among a people of unclean lips; yet my eyes have seen the King, the LORD of hosts!' (Isaiah 6.5)

So in Psalm 103 the psalmist is aware that God must be given the honour, respect and reverence which is his due. His name is holy, he is supremely special, and our response to this God in general and specifically in worship begins by recognizing that. In the psalm this special nature of God has two facets: one stresses the majesty and splendour of God, that he is 'high and lifted up' in awesome splendour, the other that he is amazingly gracious, unbelievably kind in his understanding of our frailty and generous in forgiving our sins. He is high above us, yet very near. We do not have to think of God as *either* majestic *or* loving, but as *both* awe-inspiring *and* caring. God's holiness includes both his gracious mercy and his terrifying splendour. In Psalm 103.1 and in other psalms (e.g. 33.21, 105.3, 106.47 and 145.21) God's 'holy name' is to be respected and honoured, blessed, thanked and praised out of a gratitude which has discovered the warmth and encouragement of God's love.

**Bless the LORD, O my soul,
all that is within me ...**

Psalm 103 begins and ends with an exhortation which the psalmist addresses to his whole being to respond to this holiness by worshipping God. It begins and ends with the psalmist calling upon his 'soul', 'all that is within him', his very being, to worship God.

Unfortunately we have inherited some wrong ideas about 'souls', and we have come to think that we 'have' souls. So many Christians believe that when the body dies the soul lives on and somehow floats away to be with God. We think of mortal bodies and immortal souls. Most of this was picked up from the Greek world in which the first Christians lived, and the Old Testament thinks differently. As far as the Old Testament is concerned we do not 'have' souls but we 'are' souls, or 'living souls'.

In the second creation parable in Genesis 2 God decides to make a person. He moulds the shape of this first person from the dust and then breathes into its nose the 'breath of life', and so the first man comes alive, or as the Authorized Version translates it, '... the man became a living soul' (Genesis 2.7). NRSV has 'a living being'. We do not consist of two parts added together, a body plus a soul. We are souls, or we are bodies, the two are the same thing.

Something of this has remained in our orthodox and official Christian way of thinking; for example, when we say in the Apostles' Creed that we believe in 'the resurrection of the body'. This means that when we die, we are dead, utterly and completely dead. There is no bit of us that hasn't died and which goes to be with God. We do not believe as Christians that we have immortal souls. What we do believe is that God is the creator of all life, and that he is the God of resurrection who raises the dead. So we believe that when we die he creates us anew, giving us new 'bodies', new selves, or new 'souls'. This is what that odd phrase about the 'resurrection of the body' means. It is not about dead bones coming to life again, but about God giving us new bodies or souls, 'spiritual bodies' as St Paul calls them in 1 Corinthians 15.42-44.

So at the beginning and end of Psalm 103 we are called to acknowledge and honour God with absolutely every part of our being. It is not that there is a special religious or spiritual part of us, a kind of Sunday-best bit, which prays to God and honours him in church or the like: but that every part of us, physical, mental and spiritual, or however we look at ourselves, must give God the glory due to his name.

That is the teaching, too, of the great Old Testament *Shema* prayer, so central in Judaism. After its mysterious words about God comes the command, which is endorsed by Jesus in the New Testament as the first and greatest commandment:

> You shall love the LORD your God with all your heart, and with all your soul, and with all your might.
> (Deuteronomy 6.5 and Matthew 22.36-38)

It is also repeated in that superb hymn:

> Fill thou my life, O Lord my God,
>   In every part with praise,
> That my whole being may proclaim
>   Thy being and thy ways.

Questions for reflection

1. In the common verse and response: 'Let us bless the Lord/Thanks be to God', do you think we ought to find a stronger response? If so, do you have suggestions?

2. The *Shema* refuses to name or define the God to whom we pray. What are the strengths and weaknesses of this refusal?

3. Can you think of any other or better English words than 'holy' to put across what that word is trying to say about God?

4. We do not 'have' souls – we 'are' souls. What do you think?

Conclusion

In the Introduction I admitted that Marcion had a point, and I said that the Old Testament is a vast anthology of ancient religious literature, some of which is pretty unreadable and some of which is unquestionably offensive. I did not refer to anything specific, such as Moses' command to the Israelites to engage in ethnic cleansing as soon as they entered the Promised Land by destroying its Canaanite inhabitants, or Nehemiah's demands on the returned exiles to maintain racial purity by putting away all foreign wives, to any of the numerous accounts of God punishing people, or to that vengeful cry against Babylon in Psalm 137.9 that 'Happy shall they be who take your little ones and dash them against the rock!' All of that is well enough known, so I invited you instead to look at Psalm 103.

We have read that psalm's convictions about God and the meaning of life – that life is to be lived gratefully in response to the generous God who has given it to us and blessed us in it with his steadfast love, righteousness and justice, and forgiveness – and seen how important those things are in the Old Testament itself. We have seen how the Old Testament uses important words like 'righteousness', 'judge', 'sacrifice' and 'law' in ways that are rather different to the somewhat negative ways these have been understood in Christianity down the years. We have seen that God's anger and jealousy are not quite what they seem. We have seen how the big themes in the life and work of Jesus are taken from his Old Testament scriptures – God as King and as a Father who forgives sinners. We have seen how the psalmist looks at God's generosity and 'transported with the view' is 'lost in wonder, love and praise'.

These are good reasons for reopening the Old Testament and taking the trouble to work with it and get inside it. But there is more to it than that. They also suggest that if we don't understand the Old Testament – the meaning of its words, the gist of its story and the scale of its vision – we are in danger of missing out on important testimony to the God whose name and nature is love, and on vital insight into the meaning of life, the universe and everything. They also warn us, perhaps most seriously of all, that if we don't read the Old Testament first we are in danger of misreading the New Testament and misunderstanding Jesus, and so distorting Christianity.

> Bless the LORD, O my soul,
> and all that is within me,
> bless his holy name.